CAPE WRATH TO BRORA

To Julia

Seems like a

Twin Sis Hol Plan?

C + G

2011

x

CAPE WRATH TO BRORA

A Walking Adventure Across Sutherland

Nick Lindsay

Best wishes,

Nick Lindsay.

Sunnybrae Press

Published by Sunnybrae Press
West Clyne
Brora
Sutherland
Scotland
KW9 6NH

Printed in Great Britain by Bell & Bain Ltd., Glasgow

ISBN 978-0-9563853-0-7

CONTENTS

PREFACE

Cape Wrath, in the Scottish Highland county of Sutherland, is mainland Britain's most north-westerly point. Named by raiding Vikings as their 'turning point', the Cape is now marked by a lighthouse. It was constructed in 1828 to help prevent the numerous shipping disasters which had occurred on this treacherous, exposed, wild and rugged part of the British coastline. The nearest inhabited settlement to the Cape is the small village of Durness, some 16km to the ESE and, even though there is a public road leading to the Cape, it is completely isolated from the main road network by a narrow finger of ocean known as the Kyle of Durness.

In May 2008, I undertook a solo walk from Cape Wrath, back to my home in Brora, on the east coast of Sutherland. Being no crow, *my* journey took me some 23km (14 miles) further than the direct 97km (61 mile) flying route. Camping in the wild as I went, I completed the 120km (75 mile) distance in 7 days, crossing only 3 public roads (until the last kilometre in the village of Brora), trekking through the heart of the most remote and arguably the most beautiful part of the whole country. I met with not a single soul (until, again, I was walking through the streets of my village, with less than a kilometre to journey's end) on the entire trip.

If anyone ever tells you that the Highlands of Scotland in general, and Sutherland in this particular instance, are empty and barren, then they would be so wrong or ill-informed. My journey served only to emphasise how rich and full of life and wonder the so-called 'wilderness' actually is. Almost every minute of my expedition there were different, wondrous and beautiful things to see – flora, fauna, geology, topography, meteorology, archaeology – from magnificent, immense sweeping landscapes to tiny, almost insignificant macro insects and everything in-between, but … no people. The people *were* there once, but they have now gone. Much of Sutherland is indeed empty, but in just one respect only – that of people.

I am no intrepid explorer, although I have travelled fairly extensively in my 51 years; I am no serious mountaineer, although I have frequently walked in the hills and mountains in the UK and abroad; and I am no survival expert, although I have camped and trekked in the wilds many times.

Please don't get me wrong; I am not claiming in any way that my little trek compares with any of the great adventures which probably easily spring to your mind. I am just stating that you don't have to be any of the above to have the most supreme, life-enhancing, 'Boy's Own' adventure imaginable and you don't have to travel to the ends of the earth to experience one. I am just a reasonably fit, very ordinary person who undertook a modest walk in, quite literally, my own back yard. On completing the trip, it was, perhaps, the greatest single thrill I have ever given myself and one of the most rewarding experiences of my entire life. I am still searching for ways to emulate it!

Once my journey was over and I'd reflected on each and every experience which presented itself, I just had to write it all down while it was still so fresh in my memory. I spent the spare time of the next 3 weeks after my return at the computer and the following pages are the result.

It is with some trepidation that I now expose this account of my wee adventure to a wider public; it has already been readily consumed by family and friends and, naturally enough, they have encouraged me to go this one step further. I hope you, the reader, can enjoy the story for its own sake, but I also hope that in the following pages I can convey to you the feelings I experienced and the sights I encountered over the period and give you an insight into the awe-inspiring wonders of, what has become, the place I am *thrilled* to call my home.

I now invite you to sit back, relax and read - and let *me* do the walking.

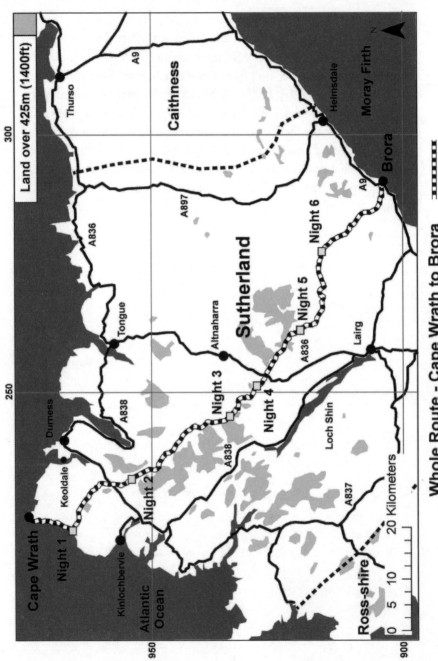

Whole Route - Cape Wrath to Brora

1

PLANNING

A terrific splash in the small, peaceful moorland river caught my attention. And there, moving effortlessly upstream, like a part-submerged mini-submarine, was a 4 foot long adult otter, thrashing about wildly when it was chasing its prey of fish. I stood on the river bank quite mesmerised, simultaneously watching and rapidly taking photographs. The otter then got out of the river, sniffed around a bit on the opposite bank, made its own distinct scent mark and slunk back into the water, before disappearing into its holt a little further upstream. I was 6 days into a 7 day solo expedition from Cape Wrath, the north-westerly tip of the British mainland, back to my home in Brora, on the east coast of Sutherland and this was the undoubted highlight of so, so many, on this great personal odyssey.

The previous week while still at home, I had seen that the weather forecasters were predicting a possible good weather window in the north of Scotland, allowing fine conditions for the second week in May (2008). I booked time off from work and flabbergasted my partner, Jacquie, when she arrived home from her work on the Friday evening to find the dining room floor strewn with camping gear in readiness for a military-style packing operation! I was intending to travel as light as I could, given that I was going to be walking around 120km, over 7 days and 6 nights.

I had always wanted to go in early May, as it can often be a good month for pleasant weather and this would also be before the dreaded midge, as well as flies and ticks, have appeared and the main obtrusive vegetation, mostly bracken, would not yet have sprung. These would be the best walking conditions, which, naturally, I was hoping for. As the forecasters had promised fine weather for the next week (we'd already had a fabulous, early May), I could afford to leave out a good deal of cold-weather gear which I would normally take on such a trip, even at this time of year. Food was to be mainly ready-made packet dried pasta dishes (evening meals), cheese and oatcakes (lunches), cereal bars (breakfasts) and dried fruit and nuts (snacks), with stream water for drinking. Cooking and camping gear formed the bulk of my load, but this was, of course, an absolute necessity.

I'd been planning to do this trip for a few years, even since before I had done a shorter, 3 day trip (Altnaharra, in Central Sutherland, to home – around 40km) 3 years previously. It hadn't been convenient to do this follow-on, longer walk until this year, so the roughly planned route was finalised after packing on the Friday evening and, the next morning - we were off! Just like that!

Sutherland is a huge (former) county, uniquely having three separate coastlines; on its west, its north and its east. The county covers the whole of the north of Scotland, apart from Caithness, which occupies the north east tip. I say former county, because none of the old counties in the Scottish Highlands *actually* exist any more – all administrative boundaries are completely different to the old county lines, so, in reality, they actually now serve no purpose at all, apart from historical. Sutherland is completely bounded to the south by the, similarly former, county of Ross-shire.

Sutherland comprises some of the wildest, rugged, spectacular and remote areas of the whole of the British Isles and, indeed, Western

Europe, and it was formerly all part of the once massive Sutherland Estate. Throughout historical times, the Sutherland family dynasty, based at Dunrobin Castle in Golspie, had owned and managed the estate; however, during the early 19th Century, the family was the architect of the notorious Sutherland Clearances. The Marquis of Stafford, who had married the sole inheritor of the estate, Elizabeth, Countess of Sutherland, used part of his own great family fortune to enhance the Estate, in readiness for the most radical changes which would upset the established, ancient way of life of the inhabitants.

The existing poor tenants were systematically evicted and the estate was divided into extensive areas for the prime purpose of becoming great sheep farms and these were leased to wealthy, incoming 'sheep barons' from the south. The motivation for this drastic upset on the part of the Sutherland Estate was purely and simply profit; it was thought that more money could be generated for the estate from the rent from the new 'improvers' than the existing subsistence tenants. These unfortunates were removed from the interior townships, into newly created crofts and villages on the coastal areas, or took themselves off as emigrees to the burgeoning colonies of the new world.

Sutherland's present population is, at around 12,500, under half of what it was in those pre-improvement days and the area largely relies on a fragile tourist industry for its existence today.

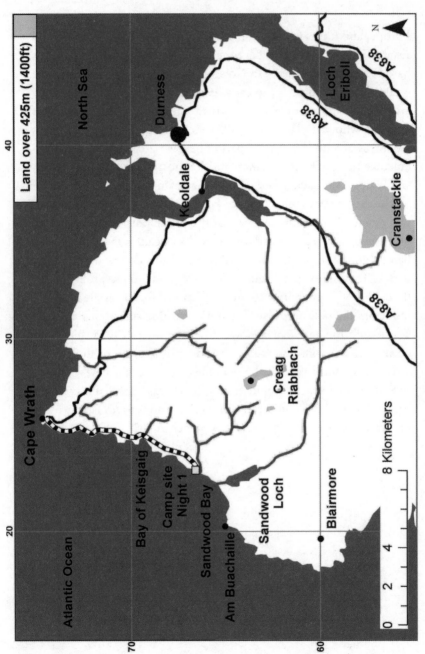

Day 1 Route - Cape Wrath to Sandwood Bay

2

DAY 1: GETTING TO THE CAPE

That excited Saturday morning, it took about 2 hours to drive from Brora to Keoldale, just south of Durness, in north-west Sutherland. Accompanying me on this vehicular leg of my trip were Jacquie and her Mum, Leoma. The weather was good as we set off, and it continued to be so, right across the county from east to west, the reverse of the journey I was about to undertake on foot. At times, what lay ahead seemed a daunting prospect. I am generally a fair-weather walker, not at all enjoying times of rain on the hill. Poor weather, in my opinion, only makes for uncomfortable and unpleasant conditions, which diminish the pleasure gained from being out in the countryside, not to mention the lack of a view, so I was quite encouraged by the early signs and the longer range forecast.

Before I could begin the walk, I had to cross the Kyle of Durness by the tiny passenger ferry at Keoldale (Plate 1) and then take an 11 mile trip in a rickety tourist minibus to its destination at the Cape Wrath lighthouse. The ferry departed at 1.45, but, in the time approaching, the gathering crowds (well, 17 of us, anyway!) were mystified where the ferry actually was. John Morrison, the ferryman, whiled away his time in his transit van, parked at the top of the small slipway, showing not the slightest sign of urgency. At 1.40, to the relief of the passengers who had reached relative fever pitch in the waiting, John leapt onto the rocks below and hauled in a wee red, open boat moored just offshore, hopped in and started its outboard engine. Surely this boat could not be the ferry? He passed the pier and the curious, onlooking waiting contingent and continued on to a boat moored further out that hardly looked any larger, but it did have a front canopy! *This* was the ferry and he brought it over to the slipway.

The canopied ferry took only 10 people at a time, so John loaded the first batch, counted those left on dry land and, worryingly, announced to the waiting seven (including me) that the minibus on the other side only took 16! The first 10, now being ferried across on the 10 minute crossing were sitting pretty, as they could obviously claim their seats in the bus for the ride to the Cape. John duly returned from the other side, loaded with 10 tourists from the morning excursion to the Cape and embarked the concerned remaining passengers into the boat. If I was the one to miss out (I was the only single person on the trip – everyone else was with a companion), then my trip could be scuppered before it had even begun – or I faced an unwelcome 11 mile walk - just to begin my trip! I, exactly like my fellow travelling companions, just had to hope I could get a seat.

From the ferry, I waved farewell to the crowds (Jacquie and Leoma) on terra firma, not only concerned about the impending mini-bus space problem, but also that I might be back in Brora before them, should they fail to successfully navigate their way back home across the county!

Once on dry land on the other side of the Kyle, all fears were finally allayed, as the bus driver announced he could fit everyone in, as long as one couple shared a single seat. At least, this would be the arrange- ment for the journey out; everyone would get a seat on the return, as I only needed a single trip on the bus. Given the tight nature of the interior of the minibus, sharing a seat didn't appear to be a very com- fortable option, so I volunteered to sit on my rucksack in the front floor-well, unconsciously gaining myself the best view in the process and also being able to talk to the driver, David Hird, who amazingly, it transpired, lived in Brora!

I didn't know David, but recognised his face from somewhere, but was quite taken aback when he said he was from my own east coast village. He stays in a caravan in Durness during the summer months while he drives the bus, coming over with the first ferry and going back on the last. In the winter, he's back in Brora with his wife and he told me he adored the lifestyle. Who wouldn't? David is no mug; a retired Constitution Lawyer, who has been the Cape Wrath minibus driver for the last 8 years, this was certainly quite a change to his former existence, and one for the better, in his opinion - and mine too!

David was an extremely informative and enthusiastic guide, as well as driver, and he took great pleasure in thrashing the minibus about on the narrow, single track road. He was totally secure in the knowledge that there would be no oncoming traffic to meet, as this road was only normally used by his minibus; the Cape is completely uninhabited. Being as close to him as I was, I could easily sense his passion for the job he now undertakes with aplomb. The road is actually a public road, although next to nobody ever drives on it, and it is one of very few routes which are completely isolated and not connected with the rest of the national network.

It was little wonder that David was so knowledgeable about the area; he was about to launch the publication of his fascinating and comprehensively researched book 'A Light in the Wilderness' the following Saturday in Durness, about the history, natural science, tourism and modern day use of the Cape, which I promised to purchase once back in civilisation.

With a small island, Garvie Island, just offshore from Cape Wrath still being used as an occasional bombing range by the Allies, part of the Cape (including the road) is off limits during the actual exercises.

Fortunately, the Armed Forces were playing somewhere else, so we had an uninterrupted, albeit bumpy ride all the way to the lighthouse, perched above some of the highest cliffs in Britain.

Cape Wrath lighthouse itself was built by Robert Stevenson, in response to 3 sinkings offshore in one storm in 1828, and a whole infrastructure had to be created for its construction and maintenance. This included the 11 mile road, as well as a jetty at Kervaig Bay, close to the lighthouse, which was used for servicing the lonely outpost until it became unmanned in 1998.

After a brief wander around the tower and a view from the fog-horn station, out to the vast expanse of ocean all around and the faint outline of Lewis in the Outer Hebrides, around 80km distant to the WSW, I asked David to take a souvenir photograph of me at the 'real' beginning of my expedition. I said farewell to him, as I hauled on my towering rucksack and set off southwards on my long trek at 3pm, leaving my fellow minibus passengers looking around the light-house site. As I did so, I wondered if they would notice, or even give a second thought to the fact that there was a person missing from the floor-well on their return to Keoldale.

3

DAY 1: CAPE WRATH TO SANDWOOD BAY

The weather was fine and sunny, although there was a cool easterly breeze and, as I wandered off southwards along the cliff-tops of some of the finest scenery in Britain, I couldn't help thinking of what might be in store for me over the next week. I was a fairly fit 51 year-old, but, would my back cope with the weight of my rucksack? Would my feet stand the pace and not come out in blisters? Would the predicted good weather hold? Would any of these reasons, or any others which hadn't even crossed my mind, force me to give up my once in a lifetime trip? Having excitedly told many people of my planned trip, I was a bit apprehensive about failure – for *any* reason!

The first kilometre was full of stops; adjusting my rucksack straps, taking an outer layer off, getting my camera out and adjusting my telescopic walking stick to the correct height. I had never used a stick before, but thought of it just before leaving Brora that morning. I popped into Cunningham's, the local hardware shop, where I had seen them on sale the previous year. No luck. All sold out, but the assistant checked with the owner, Jim Cunningham, who just happened to have one in the office, which had a cracked cowl at the end of one of the sections. This didn't affect its performance, it just wasn't saleable. On finding out what I was going to use it for and when, Jim, generously as usual, told me just to take it - I didn't realise then how much use it would be put to and how much I'd have missed it had it not been lurking in the back shop! It was overall, perhaps, my most useful accessory on the whole trip.

Possibly second on the 'most useful accessory' list was my 'bumbag'. It is something I've always worn in recent years when out on the hill, even if I am carrying my large rucksack on my back. I would thoroughly recommend the wearing of one, a large one if possible, as it allows the freedom of having all equipment required during a stroll at hand, if it is worn on the front. It negates the need to stop and take off your rucksack to get out your camera, or your binoculars, or your notebook, or your water bottle, and many other things besides. As well as these items, I also carry my compass, GPS navigation unit, maps, hand lens, pen knife, gloves and hat in it too, together with all of my day's snacky things. It seems such a simple accessory – and it is - but I've found it saves so much time, which would otherwise be taken up with taking off and putting back on your rucksack, and the associated effort and inconvenience involved too.

So, all minor adjustments made, I was properly underway this time as I glimpsed the minibus disappearing in the distance on probably the quietest public road of all. I was feeling very buoyant with the prospect of a week's total self-reliance and I thought to myself that I was glad I wasn't in that white cocoon, currently being thrown about by David on its precarious return to Keoldale. I would soon be totally alone on the Cape, except for the hardy wildlife, of which I was to see so much.

The gently rolling terrain at the top of the cliffs made for easy walking, with broad, grass and rock-strewn domes dissected by shallow valleys carrying small burns. My first photograph was taken still within sight of the lighthouse, just peeping over the short-cropped grass which was peppered with peat hags. A lovely, short Heath Spotted Orchid paraded itself with a few friends, as it sheltered from the coastal breeze. Today wasn't too bad, but you could see evidence of how life was able to survive in the harshest of conditions in the exposed places on this higher ground, as any vegetation apart from grass, such as heather, grew in a linear fashion in the lee of the many small rocks lying on the surface.

As it was already 3pm when I set off from the Cape, I didn't have very ambitious plans for covering great distances on that first afternoon. I was heading for the vicinity of Sandwood Bay, the most northerly beach on mainland Britain's west coast, around 10km to the south, which I could see, with its dominating sea stack, Am Buachaille (the Herdsman), at its south end, in the distance from the Cape. Stretching for well over a mile, the sandy bay is one of the most striking (and least frequented) beaches in Britain. It is only accessible on foot, either from Cape Wrath in the north, or, the more usual, shorter 6km route from Blairmore in the south. Either way, it is a remote spot, only reached by the hardy and the dedicated. There are long-standing tales of the bay being haunted by a bearded, shipwrecked mariner and, on September 30th 1941, during the 2nd World War, a Mk 1 Spitfire (No R7154) was forced to land on the beach after engine failure. The pilot, Sgt Kilburn was reported as *being safe*.

The plane had been a 'presentation' Spitfire, bought as part of the war effort for the RAF in 1940 by donation (commonly known at the time as the Spitfire Fund) from the people of Accrington, Church and Oswaldtwistle in Lancashire. Its first flight was on February 26th 1941, and it was based, at the time of its final forced landing, at Castletown in Caithness, as part of 124 Squadron assigned to the defence of the Orkney anchorage of Scapa Flow. Following its unscheduled appearance at Sandwood, it was struck off charge in March 1942 and abandoned where it lay, after being stripped of its valuables. From time to time parts of it appear from the shifting sands and a walker I had met at the Cape, who had just trekked up from

Sandwood, told me that one of its propeller blades and its engine had been visible that morning. Being very interested in Sutherland air crash sites, I definitely wanted to visit it and record what was left. He also told me to look out for the partly decomposed carcass of a Killer Whale, which had been washed up on the sandy beach and had been left high and dry. So that was two things of intrigue on the beach of Sandwood Bay for which it would be worth making a detour.

My first proper stop of the whole trip was a planned one. The Highland Council's Archaeology Unit in Inverness maintains a database (the Historic Environment Record – HER) of all known archaeological sites in the Highland area and I had consulted this before I set off. With a somewhat more than keen interest in archaeology, I had downloaded all of the sites I was likely to encounter on the entire route, which only numbered around 30 in total. The first one on my list was originally reported to be a fort on the promontory of Dunan Beg (HER Ref: MHG12160), which jutted out into the foamy sea hundreds of feet below, around 1.5km south of the lighthouse.

I had stopped to admire the spectacular sea arch of A' Chailleach Am Bodach a little earlier (Plate 2), sculptured from vertically orientated Lewisian Gneiss (at 2800 million years old, forming the oldest rocks in Britain) and then made my way to the promontory close by. A rickle of stones had been placed across the narrowest part where connected to the main landmass and this had been reported as a promontory fort to the Archaeology Unit in a letter by a T C Welsh in August 1972. It had also been visited by an Ordnance Survey archaeologist in 1980, who cast doubt on this interpretation, stating that the promontory had merely been isolated by a *'modern hefting dyke'* across its narrow point. I had to agree that this 10m long, 1m wide and barely 0.3m high wall constituted no fort!

Still searching for the first 'proper' archaeology on the trip, I continued south, spying a couple of Great Skuas flying about in the breeze. These great brown sea birds, with flashes of white on their underwings, are more commonly found in the northern isles, where they are known as 'bonxies', a name which has recently been adopted for their mainland cousins here in NW Scotland. The bonxie is a summer breeding visitor to these few spots in the country and is a vicious bully of a bird, scavenging food in mid flight from unsuspecting fellow birds, especially gannets, that have already caught their food and also raiding the nests of other birds for eggs and chicks. Unsuspecting walkers, too, receive the exhilarating experience of being dive-bombed when straying too close to skua nesting sites, which are just scrapes in the ground on exposed moorland.

As I watched the bonxies almost playing at their aerial acrobatics in the wind, I recalled, from my youth, trying to encourage the dive-bombing experience when walking out through their nesting areas to Muckle Flugga, on the island of Unst, the most northerly tip of Shetland. I remembered how the only way of escaping their low swoops was to cower down when under attack, and you needed eyes in the back of your head to cover all of the angles they'd appear from. Fortunately, in my experience, the skuas never drop any 'chemical' bombs; they just try to frighten you off by plunging down on you and, combined with the swooshing noise they make as they pass within inches, it certainly keeps the adrenalin going! Today, I couldn't have posed much of a threat to their nesting areas; I was left completely untroubled as I passed them just casually spying on me from the air and from the ground.

Apart from other sea birds far below on the cliffs, the only other birds I had seen so far were many Wheatears, with their distinctive white tail flash when flying and even more distinctive bobbing and clucking when standing on prominent points, and Skylarks. The latter birds are *everywhere* on the open moorland and are so much part of the background noise of this area. They sing incessantly as they rise and hover way above for ages, before their note changes to a continuous, high-pitched shrill as they glide back down to Mother Earth.

They are often so difficult to see; you can almost always hear them, but can you spot them? It's often difficult, especially as they always seem to be in the line of the sun!

More wildlife appeared on the peat hags inland. My progress was being monitored by a small herd of seven Red Deer hinds - they had interrupted their grazing to keep a wary watch on this slow-moving trespasser. As they saw I was only passing, they, too, stood their ground and then carried on their almost constant ritual of foraging for the new springtime green shoots which were now appearing on the hill. I also had my first sighting of the first of dozens of Great Black Slugs, slowly moving through the short grass and also the first of what turned out to be the most widespread flower encountered on the whole trip, the Common Dog-violet. This member of the pansy family is a beautiful ground-hugging plant, with lobe-shaped petals at the end of single stalks, its colour varying from plant to plant from a pale mauve to a dazzling, deep purpley-blue. Many places on the journey were carpeted in dog-violets and isolated examples clung to seemingly the most inhospitable places at times.

Moss Campion also made a first appearance in front of me, as an extravagant flash of pink, hugging a cushion of green beneath and clinging to rocks and sandy patches of ground. This beautiful alpine plant occurs quite commonly on the high mountains, but also down to sea level in these northern latitudes. The vivid, small pink flowers have either 4 or 5 petals which burst open, flat to the sky and the lush green moss below appears as a perfectly rounded, close-cropped spongy base layer. More upright and much less spectacular, but of just as much floral interest at this time were the sedges, which were exploding into tiny pale yellow, frilly flowers themselves, after which is left behind a conspicuous dark brown, cylindrical flower head.

I eventually crossed the first valley, Clais an Dunain, before reaching my archaeological site No 2 (HER Ref: MHG9606), which had been described by the same T C Welsh in 1972 as a structure of laid flags, measuring 9m x 6m. The later OS surveyor had modified its description to two contiguous collapsed bothies, with four adjoining lambing pens. What was now no more than a pile of stones, standing around 0.5m high, was set on a beautiful, broad, short grassy saddle, protected from the sea by a rise to the cliff top, with views to the interior of the Cape. On closer inspection, there was indeed an enigmatic structure comprising a central core of two larger chambers, now spread to around 11m x 8m, which included the four smaller satellite cells, and these were just discernible in the melee of slabs. The structure had clearly deteriorated since these two earlier visitors made their recordings, but their findings held that this was a shieling, but maybe the 'adjoining pens' were synchronous with the main original structure too.

A shieling was a small heather or turf-thatched, stone and turf building, used generally by the women and children of a township or farmstead during the summer months. In the early summer, when the crops were beginning to grow in the township, it was time to remove the few cattle and other livestock up to the ancient shieling grazing grounds, which may have been many miles away up in the hill valleys. This practice largely died out with the massive changes brought about by the Highland Clearances in the early 19th Century, but still existed in some places, such as the Outer Hebrides, during the first part of the following century.

After being left uninhabited over the winter, the men of the village would usually visit the shielings to undertake any necessary maintenance, prior to the arrival of the women and children. The men returned to the townships to tend the crops and carry out any repairs to buildings and dykes back home, while the women and children looked after the livestock at the shielings. The shieling folk took minimal supplies, which included bere (a type of barley) for making porridge and bannocks; much of the rest of their sustenance came from dairy products, made on site at the shieling grounds from the livestock, supplemented by hunted food, such as fish and maybe even venison. The shieling huts were small (barely bigger than a tent), but functional; the majority of time must have been spent outside.

The next valley to cross was Clais Lechairnich, carrying Allt na Clais Leobairnich through a great ravine for its last 500m before it reached the sea. Much flotsam and jetsam had been tossed way back from the beach into this narrow inlet, including many bits of scattered polystyrene which had been blown part way up the other side of the valley. I noted as I step-stoned across the burn, that there was a nice flat patch of grass and it flashed through my mind to use it as my resting place for the night, but, as I'd not yet even made 3km, I pressed on, to cover more ground.

By now, I was just getting into my rhythm and strode out just to the west of the dome-shaped Sithean na h-Iolaireich. More new flora presented itself, including the beautiful deep blue of the tiny flowered Heath Milkwort, the bright yellow, easily recognisable and common Bird's Foot Trefoil (which has over 70 recorded local name variants, amongst which is the delightfully nick-named Granny's Toenails!) and the upright purple-flowered thrust of Selfheal.

The geology, too, alternated between sections of the erosion-resistant Lewisian Gneiss and the relatively much softer, distinctively brown-red Torridonian Sandstone, which at around 1100 million years old, is a mere youngster compared to the ancient gneiss landscape upon which it was deposited. In this section, the cliffs were topped with weird, wind-sculptured towers of sub-horizontally bedded Torridonian and the dangerous cliff tops comprised mainly unvegetated bare sections of loose rock, sloped towards the sheer drop to the sea. I didn't venture too close to the edge! The composition of the sandstone is mainly sand grains, but it also includes many water-worn, rounded quartz and chert pebbles distributed throughout in layers. Interestingly, when the sandstone outcrops weather away, these more resistant pebbles fall out to be left strewn about like fields of marbles on the land surface. The chert pebbles, in particular, would have made a prized commodity for Stone Age man, in the absence of any local flint, with which to make tools and weapons.

This staccato start I'd made to my trip had already put me behind my provisional schedule. I had been busy observing, noting and photographing all of these things, not to mention taking 'tourist' snaps of the spectacular scenery all around. I hadn't deliberately been making a leisurely progress, it was just that there had been so much to see, to stop at and to admire, that my time seemed to evaporate right in front of me. I could imagine people asking me on my return if I was ever bored, just plodding over the land all day, every day. My answer would be a categoric no, as almost *every* minute provided a different and unique view, a different plant, a different animal, a different rock formation, or a different site of archaeological interest. Bored, I definitely was not!

Once over the crest of the hill, the previously obscured view to the south opened up again and the dramatic Bay of Keisgaig lay 400ft below. The seawater was crystal clear, and patches of sand on the bed of the bay shone through the surface like aquamarine panes in a stained glass window. Some gigantic flat slabs of sandstone had slipped down off the high cliffs and onto the massive wave-cut platform and shore and the tide was lapping about their sides. Their position and enormous size made them resemble the concrete sections of the Mulberry Harbour, which were towed across the Channel to Arromanches in Normandy after the D-Day invasion in June 1944 and anchored to form a temporary floating harbour for the Allies to unload their vital supplies.

I had been quite looking forward to reaching this point, which was only around half-way to Sandwood. The next archaeological site had been recorded on the HER (Ref No: MHG17964) as '*what may be an unroofed building*', but it had never been visited archaeologically; the information had been added by the Royal Commission on the

Ancient and Historical Monuments of Scotland (RCAHMS), when noticed by them on the OS 1st edition map of 1878. Peering down into the bay far below, I spotted the building remains perched precariously high up on the southern bank of the Keisgaig River. The building was aligned parallel to the burn (small river) and perpendicular to the shoreline and was situated on a lofty patch of coastward-sloping grass surrounded by heather, only yards from the rocky beach. Carefully negotiating my way down the craggy slope of the cliffs to the Keisgaig River's north bank, I crossed the burn into the parish of Eddrachillis and made for the building remains.

I was surprised to discover, on arrival at the building, that the landward part of the structure had been roofed with growing heather and turf. The organic roof was supported by driftwood timbers straddled across the tops of its sandstone block walls and a narrow way in led from the centre of the uphill side. No one was at home; in fact no-one lived there on a permanent basis now, but it had no doubt been used as shelter on occasion in relatively recent times, as evidenced by an empty half-bottle or two lying about on the damp, but cosy inside. I couldn't actually stand up inside, as the roof was so low, but there would have been enough room for a couple of people to lie down to weather out a night or two.

I was the first to have visited the site archaeologically, which always gives me a bit of a thrill! It clearly shows how much opportunity there is in this part of the country for genuine exploration of parts of a landscape that hasn't been trodden on for 200 years or so, if, indeed, at all. There is still much yet to discover out there and I have always felt very privileged to have done this; I know it's not like reaching the South Pole or climbing Everest, but it is still frontier exploration of a sort, of a realistically achievable nature, and available for anyone.

Having recorded and photographed the former dwelling site, I set off up the steep south valley side at almost 7.00, once more aiming south-west along the cliff-tops and across the coastal wilderness. Again the sandstone cliffs were dissected by deep, narrow ravines which penetrated only short distances inland, affording spectacular views down to the rock and the sea far below. One of these ravines formed a huge crevasse between amazing knife-sharp, serrated promontory ridges on either side, which I *didn't* traverse along to investigate! Riding on the calm ocean surface, I spied a pair of kayakers paddling about at the base of the cliffs and thought to myself that they would have a pleasant and easy ride back to Sandwood, where presumably they would be camping.

An old line of rusty iron fence posts emerged at the top of this same ravine and turned to run parallel to the cliffs, set back about 20m from the top. Its wires had become detached long ago through a combination of corrosion, weather and animal wear and tear, and dated from a time when boundaries in this part of the world were obviously more important than they are today. From the top of the next, un-named, rounded, rocky Torridonian sandstone hill there was a clear view across to Sandwood Bay, by then only around 3km away. A stone cairn, casually built by passing walkers over the years at this prominent spot, had been constructed from many of the large slabs of sandstone which lay strewn about the surface. A single huge boulder of contorted Lewisian gneiss was also resting on the same bedrock nearby, but this had been left stranded by the receding glacier which carried it to its final destination at the end of the last Ice Age, around 10,000 years ago.

It was now 7.40 and I could see my destination of Sandwood clearly in front of me. Having seen the kayakers earlier, I figured that the Bay may well be populated with many weekend campers, so I decided to search for a site on which to pitch my tent, far from the potential madding crowd, before reaching the Bay itself. As my tired legs carried me down the south slope of Cnoc a' Gheodha Ruiadh (Hill of the Red Cove), I was faced with wondering where to cross the final burn of the day, the Strath Chailleach River (the River of

19

the Glen of the Old Woman). It lay a couple of hundred metres away from me and I could see there was no obvious crossing point. I didn't want a massive inland detour at this time of the evening, so I gambled and headed for its downstream end, thinking I could always wade across the river, if necessary.

As I approached the river's coastal termination, I spotted a small, flat, short grass and heather-covered area, surrounded by a low ring of Lewisian bedrock. The platform was only just larger than the size of a single tent, which was just going to be absolutely ideal. I could not have wished for a better, more stunning site, overlooking the beautiful, clean sandy beach below, just north of the main part of Sandwood Bay, with a perfect view down the whole length of the Bay itself and out across the open sea of The Minch to the west (Plate 3). My water supply was the river about 50m away, which, as it tumbled down to the beach below, was choked with large boulders, and these would make ideal stepping stones to cross tomorrow.

I had, indeed, landed both on my feet and also in heaven, and quickly set about pitching my tent and cooking my dried pasta meal. I ate it while watching the sun set on a flat calm sea, reflecting on the first day of my own fantastic adventure and wondering what tomorrow would bring at Sandwood. This first day, whilst never being totally sunny and always with a cool easterly breeze had, nevertheless, been *totally* idyllic. It had been capped superbly with the majestic setting of this perfect camp site, a lovely, welcome meal and the accompanying stunning sunset. All was very well in my little expeditionary world and I crawled into my sleeping bag in a state of complete and utter contentment.

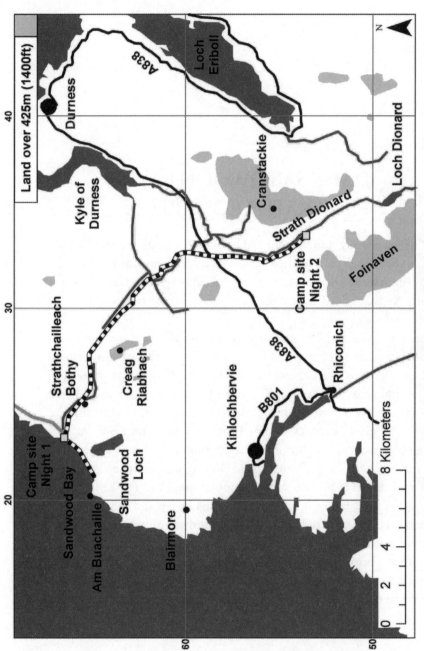

Day 2 Route - Sandwood Bay to Strath Dionard

Land over 425m (1400ft)

4

DAY 2: SANDWOOD BAY TO SRATH DIONARD

The first night in the tent had been pretty comfortable. I had not been at all cold, but had been woken a few times during the night by the rattling noise made by the wind flapping the lower part of my tent fly-sheet door against the gas cylinder of my camping stove, in the bell canopy. In the morning, I vowed to leave the stove outside the tent in future! The morning was beautiful. The sun was out and there was much blue sky, however, there was still that cool easterly breeze in the air, just to remind me it was still May and pretty early in the Highland calendar year. The views to the south were magnificent – the great length of Sandwood Bay stretched away into the distance and the giant sea stack of Am Buachaille rose from the sea, just offshore from the high cliffs at the far end of the bay. The stack is a favourite with crazy climbers, since having first been conquered by Tom Patey in 1967. The stack was not for me; I had a plane to catch!

After my camping breakfast of a multigrain bar and coffee, I left my tent set up and walked down towards Sandwood, around 1km to the south-west, crossing the Strath Chailleach River over the convenient boulders below my campsite. I photographed my first encounter with the frequently occurring, distinctive, pink-flowered Lousewort, as I made my way over great whaleback ridges of gneiss, interspersed with deep gullies, in this typical Lewisian coastal landscape. Along one of the sides of these ridges, I came across a small pod of dull grey haematite, an oxide of iron, in a pegmatite (a granitic vein) which had intruded into its host rock from deep beneath the surface around 400 million years ago. Haematite is commercially mined in many parts of the world as the main ore of iron, but this was just a small deposit. I added a small sample of it to the two chert pebbles, weathered out of the Torridonian sandstone, I'd collected yesterday. I was supposed to be *shedding* weight over the duration of the trip with the gradual consumption of my food, not adding to it!

I was very glad I'd made the decision to set up camp where I did the previous night, as I thought to myself that this rapidly undulating terrain would have really tired me out – and I didn't find a spot which would have bettered my campsite anyway. I looked back to where my tent was still pitched and it looked tiny, dwarfed as it was by the massive, slabby outcrops of gneiss, looking like giant grey blisters on a carpet of green.

Moss Campion abounded in this territory in broad, low clumps on the ground and Mountain Avens grew in a scattered formation on the short coastal grass, as I clambered down the final sandy face onto the extensive beach of Sandwood Bay below. Sandwood Estate has been in the ownership of the John Muir Trust since 1993, and the estate boundary runs along the north east side of Sandwood Loch and encompasses the whole of the main part of the beach. The Trust is a charity, whose aims are the protection of wild land for the people and for the flora and fauna, the restoration of wild lands (where they have been damaged) and the simultaneous promotion of these wild lands. Sandwood Bay and the rest of the estate, which includes the crofting townships of Sheigra, Blairmore and Oldshoremore to the south, appear to be in good hands.

Crossing into the estate over the shingle bed of the river, which flows the short distance into the sea from Sandwood Loch, trapped behind the dunes at the back of the beach, I rose onto the undisturbed sand of the bay itself. I wondered where the Spitfire remains might be and regretted not having asked the walker I'd met at Cape Wrath exactly where the wreckage was located on this mile-long extent of pure sand. The tide was also half way in, so I also speculated that it might already be below the encroaching high water mark.

Much to my disappointment, I never did find the plane, but, around two-thirds the way to the far end, I did come across the remains of the mature, male Killer Whale (it was *clearly* a male!), which had been either washed up onto the shore already dead or had become stranded there (Plate 4). It lay on its side, parallel to the length of the bay, and I recalled seeing an article about a fortnight earlier regarding the ill-fated creature in the local weekly Sutherland newspaper, the Northern Times. The 'Raggie', as the paper is affectionately known locally, reported that there had only been 11 other reported strandings of Killer Whales in the whole of Scotland over the previous 16 years, so this was quite an unusual occurrence. The report went on to state that these whales fed on fish, octopus and squid, as well as birds, seals, sharks and even other whales, and males live to around 60, although, for females, the natural lifespan is around 90 years.

Having never seen a whale in the (rotting!) flesh before, it wasn't quite as big as I thought it might be, although it had been decomposing for a while now and had obviously lost some of its bulk. It was 9m long (which, I suppose, is big enough!) and its tail sinews were exposed at this stage of decomposition. There were also some holes in its sides, where it had been pecked at by sea birds and its central area had collapsed under its own weight, being out of its natural briny habitat.

I was mostly fascinated by its large, pointed teeth, which *were* enormous! They were 6, maybe 7cms long and several of its front set were missing, having been already extracted by previous souvenir hunters and I attempted to collect one too. Largely ignoring the smell, which was strangely only really prevalent at quite close quarters, I honed in on the closest tooth and was encouraged to find that it was very loose. It was just like when you had a wobbly tooth as a youngster and you spent hours wiggling it to try to make it come out, so you could claim sixpence from the tooth fairy, or, in unbeknown reality, your Mum and Dad! The Orca's tooth wiggled and wiggled, but I just could not get a strong enough grip around it to detach it from its roots.

Some of the other souvenir hunters before me had had similarly frustrating problems and had tried bashing the teeth with a large pebble; the fallacy of this mode of attack was obvious in the shattered remains lying scattered around and the fractured remnants left attached to the poor creature's jaw. Not wanting to employ this, almost vandalistic, method of dental extraction, I reluctantly gave up and left the whale in peace.

I continued on to the end of the bay in my vain search for the Spitfire, before returning back along the tide-line, still hunting for the remains of the stricken aircraft. Maybe the wreckage had already been covered by the incoming tide and was located just above to the low water mark; after all, this is where the firmest sand would be if the tide was out at the time of its forced landing in 1942. All, however, had not been wasted on my visit - I *had* seen the whale and also I'd had a nice exploratory wander along the beach, without seeing a single soul, in contrast to my 'fears' of the previous day that it would be like Blackpool!

I headed back towards my campsite, taking a more direct, inland trek than the roller-coaster route over the gullies and ridges taken on the way out. This made not only for easier walking, but also, I hoped, for a quicker return. However, the best laid plans, and all that! As I ascended the steep, sandy face rising from the north end of the bay, I first spotted some Thrift, a common seaside floral inhabitant. It was growing in communal clumps, just like Moss Campion, whose flowers are similarly a vivid pink. Barely a couple of hundred metres from the beach, on the coast side of the highest point, was the stone outline of a shieling, which didn't appear on any archaeological database or map. As I stated earlier, this, to me, is real exploration, albeit small beer to most. No-one had publicly recorded this ancient structure and, quite possibly, no-one had ever recognised it as such, even if anyone had actually wandered past it. It was the first time for it to be studied, photographed and surveyed, and this is what makes an adventure like this so fascinating; every step of the way in this part of the country always has the possibility of revealing something new, interesting and unexplored.

The shieling was set on a gentle coast-sloping area of short-cropped grass and its walls were comprised of large, single boulders, many of which were still set on end in the ground, arranged as a continuous, lozenge-shaped shell, measuring 8m by 5m. Some of the stones had tumbled from their original upright position and now lay fallen longways on the ground and, exposed on its downslope, north east rounded corner, the walling stones were supported by a curving foundation layer of large stones poking out from the ground. The interior was fairly level in its lower part and slightly sloping down to the centre at its upper part.

The structure had been well engineered, rather than loosely arranged and was of a style I hadn't really come across before. It wasn't too similar to the jumbled shieling I'd seen yesterday, as it had nowhere near the amount of stone involved in its construction. This one had a 0.5m wide entrance on its east side, marked by the largest upright at 0.75m high, and a 1.2m x 2.5m annexe extended for 2m from its west, upper side. This annexe was not as substantial as the main structure, being delineated by a single row of smaller stones lying almost flush with the ground surface and a large, single 'lintel' stone at its western gable end. It wasn't clear if this annexe was actually originally attached to the main structure or was a separate unit entirely, used maybe as a store. One odd thing about this former building, was that it was not adjacent to a water supply, which is normally an important factor in the siting of a shieling.

It was now 11.15 and I really needed to press on; however, just over the next small gully was a beautiful patch of grazing running along the eastern side of a small burn, being attended to by several sheep. It looked ripe for more archaeology and sure enough, a 1m wide and 0.5m high, heather-topped turf and stone boundary dyke separated the grazing from the heathery area beyond. The dyke, with a shallow ditch on its eastern side, preventing water flowing onto the grassy area, extended for around 150m from almost the top of the gully. It ran to the break of slope, where the wee burn tumbled down towards the sea. Maybe this had been the grazing associated with the shieling, which was around 400m to the south west. There was no sign of any structure within the grazing area, which, given the lateness in the morning, was probably a blessing for me!

I had no further interruptions on my trip back to the tent, apart from getting what I thought was another glimpse of Lewis in the cloudy murkiness far out to sea. I looked again a few minutes later and Lewis had apparently moved! I got my binoculars out to look more closely and identified a mega-super-tanker which appeared to hog the whole horizon. It was almost unbelievably long and it was little wonder I thought it could well have been a landmass!

I arrived back at the tent at 11.45, packed up everything and headed inland, waving goodbye to the coast. I had been distracted this morning with my partially successful detour to Sandwood, which had taken up the whole of the morning and I was a little concerned that this would undoubtedly hinder my progress for the day. I had originally hoped to make my second camp somewhere on the shores of Loch Dionard, around 10km to the south east, across the other side of the A838 Rhiconich to Durness road, but this looked to be a wee bit ambitious now.

I followed the Strath Chailleach River up its north bank and crossed over at a shallow shingle rapid. The terrain was a great expanse of open, exposed moorland, in front of a range of hills with big corries, around 4km inland. This, I thought to myself, was just one relatively small drainage basin, but it appeared so vast, stretching out in front of me. It made me feel quite small and it also emphasised to me that there was an enormous distance to cover before I reached my final destination of home - and I hadn't made much progress up to then!

The moorland bog was tinder dry, as no rain had fallen for a few weeks, and the moss and lichen made an eerie, crispy, crunching noise underfoot. Attached to the tops of many of the reeds which grew out of the moorland were silver discs, a bit bigger than the size of a £2 coin and a little bit thicker. These were the nests of Garden Spiders and literally littered the landscape from here right the way across to the east coast, as I was to find out. More Heath Spotted Orchids grew out of what normally should have been soggy bogland and, in isolated lochans which hadn't completely evaporated, Bogbean was proudly craning its stems tipped with small, hairy, white, five-petalled flowers, out of the remaining dark, peaty water.

By 12.50, I'd reached what had been recorded by the Royal Commission from the OS map of 1878 on the HER (Ref No: MHG17966), as a Farmstead and discovered that it was actually a habitable bothy, maintained on behalf of the Keoldale Estate by the Mountain Bothies Association (MBA). This organisation looks after and maintains many remote bothies with the blessing of individual estates and landowners, mainly throughout Scotland, for the benefit and shelter of walkers.

I opened the outside-bolted door and entered to find that it was quite a comfortable two-roomed bothy, with a sleeping room and a sitting room. I use the word 'comfortable' as a relative term – there are no beds to sleep in or sofas to sit on, just a raised wooden platform in the sleeping room and a rickety chair or two and a small wooden table in the sitting area. It did have a fireplace, which is a must for a cosy, warming blaze at the end of what can often be a cold and wet Highland day. Walkers usually use these bothies as a single night stopover and leave them exactly as they find them, maybe adding to the peatstack or locally gathered timber pile for use of the next person.

Strath Chailleach bothy has an interesting story attached to it, which is recorded on its wall inside. One James Macrory Smith, commonly known as 'Sandy', stayed as a recluse in the bothy for around 30 years from the mid 1960s. Originally from Glasgow, he was one of 16 children of a Clydeside ship-worker, and he just liked the quiet life – how he arrived in such a place is not stated. He apparently lived well here, partly off the land and partly from bringing in supplies from Kinlochbervie, where he would walk the 20km return to collect his pension and goods every week, in good weather or bad. There was plentiful peat all around and good fishing in the river.

When his gable end collapsed in 1981, the MBA agreed to reconstruct it, providing Sandy gave his blessing for half of his home to be used as a bothy for walkers. After the reconstruction, Sandy just couldn't get used to sharing his dwelling and this invasion of what had previously been his privacy forced the termination of the agreement. However, in 1994, the solitary and hardy existence was becoming too much even for Sandy and he abandoned Strath Chailleach for a caravan at the pier in Kinlochbervie, where he remained until he died in 1999. Some of Sandy's cave-art-like wall paintings still adorn the interior walls of the bothy as a permanent reminder of his presence. The MBA rekindled their interest in the vacated bothy and had, by June 1999, restored it for the use of more traditional itinerant recluses.

After signing the visitors' book, I decided to have lunch further on when I'd made more progress. The sun was beating down at this part of the day and sheltering from the east wind was impossible in the great open space. I was heading for the Bealach Coire a' Chuidhe, which would be the first high pass of the trip and once I was over the other side, I thought that it should be plain sailing for a while downhill. After recording a possible grass and heather-covered stone cairn on this otherwise featureless sweep of land between the Strath Chailleach River and the Bealach, I had lunch in the shelter of a large Torridonian sandstone boulder, beneath the dramatic crags of Creag nan Gobhar (Crags of the Branching River). I had a scout around for a shieling, which had also been recorded on the HER (Ref No: MHG17965) by the Royal Commission from the 1878 OS map, without success, before heading up the steep approach to the Bealach. I made the top at 3.00, after a cooling and refreshing drink from the small burn on the west side of the Bealach, which at around 300m was, thankfully, going to be the highest elevation of the day.

The top was a bit of a milestone, as it was the first watershed crossed, and it also was the parish boundary between Eddrachillis and Durness, into which I had now walked again. From here, I was able to get my first mobile phone signal. This, in a way, was a bit disappointing. In reality, I wanted to do the whole trip without seeing or speaking to anyone, but, mindful of the safety implications and those at home worrying (unnecessarily, in my mind!) about me falling off a cliff or something, I owed it to them to report in when I could. I duly did this, then immediately encountered my first amphibian on the trip – a Common Frog, with its dark mottling on its mustard coloured skin. It must have been one of many which rely on the many dark, Bogbean-infested lochans scattered throughout the peat hags on the top of the Bealach. I ambled leisurely south-eastwards down the 4km long, gently sloping valley of the Allt na Creige Riabhach (River of the Greyish Crags). It spread out in front of me like a great big, khaki wilderness, with tinges of brighter green speckling the sinuous line of the burn itself, before it joined the Grudie River, which then flowed on into the south end of the Kyle of Durness.

I stopped for a fresh drink from the Grudie River, which had quite deeply incised into the deep peat and I just managed to cross it on a small shingle run above its meeting with the Allt na Creige Riabhach, without getting wet. I was making for a circular stone sheepfold I'd spotted on my way down towards the Grudie River, and within a few minutes I was there. It had been built on a small grassy shelf, next to the Amhainn ar Loin on its south west side and, although it appeared on the 1878 map, it had not been recorded on the HER. Incidentally, the burn itself was quite slow-moving at this point and in one of its small, quiet creeks there were great orangey-rusty coloured algal blooms accumulating underwater, like clouds from a Martian atmosphere.

Circular sheepfolds date from the post-Clearance period, just less than 200 years ago, when sheep took the place of the removed population of people in the hills. This one had an internal diameter of 13m and its turf and heather-topped stone walls stood partly preserved at its original 1.5m height. Its 0.5m wide and 1m high entrance faced towards the south east and it was capped by a large stone lintel, but there were no sheep using it today.

From miles away, I had already spotted the remains of a roofless building, across the valley from the sheepfold. Its walls still stood to full height, in front of grassy slopes which were being grazed by a small flock of sheep. It couldn't have been many decades ago that this farmstead, Balloch, was habited (Plate 5). This, too, was not on the HER, although it was very prominent on the map. I wasn't so keen to visit it, as it was a bit of a detour to reach it, being set part way up the hill on the other side of this wide valley; however, I did persuade myself that I ought to visit it. It had a modern post and rylock fence running just off its front side, in which, unfortunately, a now dead ram had become entangled in it by its especially curly set of horns. It would have been a particularly gruesome death, being trapped, head down, on a fence. I could just imagine its vain struggles to free itself, before it must have given up with complete exhaustion, its fate realistically sealed as soon as its horns had become first stuck.

I explored and recorded the ruin, which comprised two sections, both with thick stone side-walls standing 2m high. The south east section was the main area of habitation, as there was a fireplace on this side of the dividing wall between the sections. The north west section had a slightly lower roof (the roof-line was still evident on the north west side of the dividing wall) and must have been a store or byre. The small front-only-facing window spaces still had their lintels intact and much of the stone had been colonised by the spectacularly bright yellow lichen, Caloplaca.

As I left Balloch, no more than 60m to its south east, I discovered that the farmstead's inhabitants were not the first to occupy this green hillside swathe. What turned out to be the only example of a hut circle I encountered on the entire trip, was now no more than a circular grass-covered ridge, 1-2m wide and 0.4m high, which were the original foundations of an Iron Age roundhouse, dating to around 2000 years ago. Its internal diameter was 11m, and its walls would have stood to a metre or so, above which would have been a conical thatched roof supported by a wooden frame, rising to 5 or 6m high. Hut circles are commonly found throughout the Highland hills and glens, and are often characterised by large boulders set in the circle; however, this one had no sign of stonework whatsoever. It was set on the same gentle, south west-facing grassy slope as Balloch farmstead, an ideal spot for Iron Age farmers to grow their subsistence crops.

As I left the hut circle, it was 6.45 and I needed, as ever, to press on. It was another kilometre on a gentle rise to reach the top of the next pass, Am Bealach, which was to overlook an early significant psychological point of my walk. At 7.00, on the top, I peered down to the A838 Rhiconich to Durness road in the valley far below, and just marvelled at the sight in front of me. Appearing as though it had been incised by a massive rake, a row of 20 or more closely spaced deep gullies ran down the grassy hill in front of the impressive rocky massif of the Beinn Spionnaidh ridge high above. To its south stood the towering, 801m high Cranstackie, absolutely dwarfing the tiny white speck of the farm of Rhigloter. The farm nestles at the back of the low ground of the valley floor and its prominent long and winding track leads to it from the A838, across the entire boggy expanse of Srath (it *is* 'Srath' on the map, in this instance and not 'Strath') Dionard. And on the south side of the Srath was the even more impressive Foinaven range, largely made up of massive 600 million year old Cambrian Quartzite slabs and perhaps the most impressive scree slopes anywhere in Scotland. This panorama marked the end of the western section of my trip and the beginning of the extensive central part. Plain sailing to my camp for tonight from here, I thought!

I strode across the steep grass and heather-covered slope, down towards the public road, hoping not to stumble on any more archaeology. There was nothing in this area that I'd previously selected to visit but, sure enough, stumble on archaeology, I did! On a beautifully smooth, grazed grass-covered area, way above the building called Carbreck at the side of the A838, there was a low, stone-walled enclosure adjacent to a small burn. There was no sign in the vicinity of habitation, so I quickly recorded the small structure and continued on obliquely down to the road, where a couple of cars passed me by. I crossed the tarmac and carried on across the valley floor towards the River Dionard. What would normally have been quite boggy ground was, again, largely very dry, but it was very hummocky and awkward to walk over. Not really what was required at this time of what had been quite a tiring day. By now it was after 8.00 and the light was beginning to fade. No such luxury of having a sunset over the sea as I'd had the night before! The sun had long since disappeared from the valley floor, although it still shone brightly on the high peaks in front of me, making for quite a special sight.

Once on the bank of the River Dionard, I followed it upstream. I had considered crossing over to the other side, taking out a bend in the river, however, there was no place suitable to cross without wading, so I stuck to the west bank. The walking was now not comfortable at all, as the river bank was constantly dissected with small gullies and the heather was deep and overgrown in between. Eventually, after passing a river-watcher's hut, the recently improved stony vehicle track I'd been looking forward to intercepting came into view. It was a relief to do some pacier walking, although I did feel a wee twinge of a possible blister on the sole of my left foot as I marched out on the contrasting hard surface of the track. This threw some alarming thoughts into my mind about the feasibility of 5 more days walking with this potential impediment.

I continued along the track, looking for the first suitable place to camp, as it was around 8.30 by now. On I walked, past another river-watcher's hut, checking out a site or two, which I found not to be good enough – the site had to be a combination of being close to the river, on a nice flat patch of grass or heather and, most importantly, sheltered from that incessant, cold easterly wind. I was always looking for the perfect site, but time was running out; soon, I'd have to be less choosy, and set up camp wherever I could. Past a third hut and still looking. Then, as if my own St Christopher was looking over me, the route of the former track departed from the new, improved one and hugged the river bank at a bend in its course. I took a look and all my ideal criteria were fulfilled at once. On a narrow, flat terrace of the river bank, the old, disused grassed-over track had cut deeply through a peat bank. It was ideal; flat, grassy and sheltered – all in one spot.

To the huge relief of my shoulders, I took off my rucksack and quickly set about putting up my tent. By 9.40, the tent was erected and I was cooking my pasta a bit later than planned, but it didn't really matter. I'd had a good day, crossed two watersheds, as well as the A838 and had left the west coast well behind. I felt pleased about my progress, even though I'd only done 17km as the crow flies. I reckoned from the map I had actually done about 20km, which didn't include the 5km round trip at the start of the day to the south end of Sandwood Bay and back from my campsite.

My only concern about this site, as I pitched the tent and later lay in my sleeping bag, was that it was obviously used frequently by Red Deer, as there were hoof prints in the peat and droppings all about. It was a bit of a calculated gamble staying there, as I pessimistically imagined that I could be trampled in my sleeping bag overnight! There were no obstacles lying around in the vicinity that I could place in the way, to prevent the large beasts coming through on their normal pathway. I just had to hope that they would use their powerful senses of smell and sight to detect that something out of the ordinary lay in their normal route, because at the very least if one, or even a few, came through in the night, the tent, if not me, would surely suffer some irreparable damage! These were my final thoughts as I drifted off to sleep at 11.00, to the comforting sounds of the babbling river about 2m to my side.

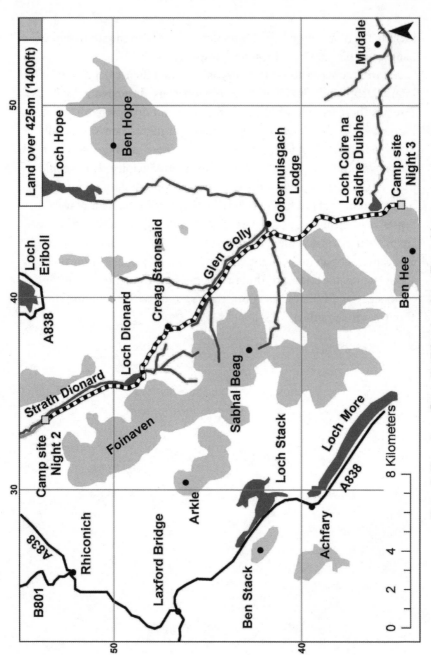

Day 3 Route - Strath Dionard to Ben Hee ░░░░░░░

Land over 425m (1400ft)

Camp site Night 2 ▫

Camp site Night 3 ▫

0   2   4   8 Kilometers

5

DAY 3: SRATH DIONARD TO BEN HEE

I did wake up alive, thankfully untrampled and unbothered by any marauding beasts, but I wasn't completely trouble free. As I lay there in my sleeping bag, happy to have been spared, my legs were telling me that someone had spent all night pounding them from top to bottom with a rubber mallet or, at least, that's how it felt! Yesterday morning when I got up, my legs had been tired, but this morning they were sore! Anyway, a brisk walk would soon sort that out, I thought!

Again, the weather that morning was glorious, better, in fact, than yesterday. The sun was warm at 8.30 when I convinced my legs to come out of the relative comfort of their sleeping bag. I had breakfast perched on a rock above the river and all was well in my own little solitary world; even my legs felt less weary in the magnificent riverside surroundings, dominated by the high rocky slopes of Cranstackie.

When planning the journey at home, I had wanted to climb Cranstackie, not just because it is a very accessible and spectacular mountain, but because it also has the remaining wreckage of a De Havilland Mosquito aircraft, which crashed just below the top of the peak on April 5th 1943. It was on a bombing exercise from RAF Skitten in Caithness, in preparation for a 'Highball' bombing raid on the German Ruhr dams, planned as one of the associated raids the day before the famous 'Dambuster' raids. Something must have gone tragically wrong and both members of the crew, the Pilot, Flying Officer Donald Pavey and the Navigator/Air Bomber, Sergeant Bernard Stimson, were killed instantly in the accident. On this occasion, I reluctantly decided not to try and locate the site because I was already slightly behind schedule on my trek. The detour up Cranstackie would probably have taken the majority of the day, given that I didn't know exactly where on the mountain the wreckage was and I also had rather a large load on my back to haul up the full extent of the mountain's steep slope. I did return, however, a couple of weeks later to complete this unfinished business and located the wreckage of the plane, strewn over a couple hundred metres of the steep north west face, about 170 metres below the summit.

So, decision made, tent packed and it was off again at 10.00, wondering where my journey would take me today. It was taking me around an hour and a half to get away in the mornings, from getting up to getting underway. This seemed to me to be quite a long time, but there was a lot of methodical, organised packing to be done, and I suppose I was taking quite a time relaxing over my breakfasts in their spectacular and extraordinary settings. Over the trip, I was to cut the time taken in the morning to just over the hour, which wasn't too bad in the end.

At home, I had planned to aim for a small loch, called An Gorm Loch, as my next campsite, about 5km west of the next public road (the A836 connecting Lairg and Tongue), but I wasn't sure if I'd make that now. Continuing along the valley floor of Srath Dionard on the improved Gualin Estate fishing track, I was pleased to feel that my feet were coping well and there was no sign of the supposed blister I was feeling last night. After around a kilometre of walking, being mesmerised by the stunning scenery all around in this deep, U-shaped glacial valley, I came across the shieling I'd identified on the

HER (Ref No MHG17912), which again, had only been recorded from the OS map of 1878.

Situated on the north west side of Allt Coire Duail, which flows down from Foinaven's Coire Duail and on the north east side of the track, the distinctive shieling was the shape of a 'D' on the ground, measuring around 5m x 4m. Its boulder walls stood around 40-50cms high and were now spread to around 1m wide and its interior was marked by tall reeds. Its north east frontage was the face with angular corners, and this was also where its narrow, 30cms wide entrance was centrally placed; the rear south west face had rounded corners. The interior space was tiny, as with most shielings; this one was only 2.4m x 2m. I left the old shieling, which had been a summer dwelling probably for a single small family, marvelling at the resilience of the people who made it their temporary home and the location in which it was set, and carried on towards Loch Dionard and the end of the formalised track.

As ever, there was an abundance of the pretty, pink-flowered Lousewort growing in the moorland on either side of the track and, in the track's cut peat sides, there was evidence of the dominant vegetation of former times. Stumps and attached roots of fir trees are commonly found all over the Highlands in the peat, and here was no exception. These stumps are all that remain of the original Caledonian Pine Forest (apart from a few still surviving, still growing localised pockets) which almost completely carpeted the Highlands a few thousand years ago, similar to Alpine slopes today. With a combination of a warming climate and man depleting it for fuel and building materials, the forest has largely disappeared and all that remains are these stumps buried deep in the peat. They are often found in peat cuttings and one, extracted from the peat in Rogart, on the east side of Sutherland in 1994, has on it, what have been identified as Bronze Age axe cuts, dating to around 2000BC.

Just before reaching the loch, a modern wooden bridge carried the track over Allt Coire na Lurgainn. The dominating backdrop to this spot was the soaring, spectacular scree-covered ridge of A Ch'eir Ghorm, connected to the south east end of Foinaven. The water flowing down from the Alpine-like high corrie was crystal-clear, and its clarity was exaggerated even more by the fact that the river bed consisted of white Cambrian quartzite boulders and pebbles (Plate 6). The icy cold water itself was so pure, tasty and very refreshing to drink. I have to say that all of the water I drank on the entire trip tasted very good, even when it was peat-stained brown, but I think this was just about the best. Whether this water tasted so good because it was a psychological result of it looking so fresh and inviting to drink, I wasn't sure, but the sight of the water, the burn and the surroundings certainly made for a good, all round experience!

Once across the bridge, the beautiful, deep blue Loch Dionard came into view. There was a wooden milepost at the side of the track, erected by the estate to inform fishermen that they were 6 miles from Gualin House and the A838. The track stopped at a small, modern fishing hut on the north west end of the loch and I made my way round the loch's south west side, close to the towering, bare rock, almost sheer slopes of Creag Urbhard (Plate 7), a huge massif of shiny grey rock and scree. Many boulders had fallen from these slopes over thousands of years and had come to rest on the peaty ground above the shoreline. Some are *just* enormous and are covered with their own fascinating, mini eco-system, which incredibly include a thick peat base, in which grows a luxuriant crop of the usual flora found on the ground: moss, heather, bilberry and lichen (Plate 8).

On the other side of the loch, an old farmstead called Carrachandubh, which still appears on the current edition of the OS map, was a tempting visit, but there was nowhere to cross the river at the north end of the loch without wading, so my present route had effectively been dictated to me. However, all was not lost as there was also some known archaeology, 'an unroofed building', recorded on the HER (Ref No MHG18805), half way along the loch-side I was taking.

This, too, had not been visited, only recorded by the RCAHMS from the OS 1st edition map, but it had disappeared from the map by the time of the subsequent edition in 1908.

On a patch of grass which had formed on the lower part of a small alluvial fan at the side of the loch, there were, indeed, the remains of a small, rectangular stone building. The fan had been created over the millennia by debris carried by a small burn which falls, in two stages, from the high rock slabs above, in a narrow but spectacular broken waterfall. The wall footings of the building stood less than 0.5m high at its highest point (the north gable end), with the rest of the walling being marked by a line of single quartzite boulders, around the size of a football or slightly larger. The footings measured 6.5m × 2.8m and its longsides ran down the slope, so that its north gable end faced the loch. This would have been a lovely spot at which to live!

Only 7m away from the building's east side lay a shieling, and this one had *not* been marked on the map or recorded on the HER. All that remained was its low, round-topped, grass-covered walls of peat, standing only 30cms high. It was lozenge-shaped, with rounded corners, its external dimensions were only 5m x 3m and it was orientated downslope, similarly to its adjacent stone-walled neighbour. Being this small externally, its interior measured only 3.5m x 2m; the shielings in this part of the county were getting smaller! It was unclear whether these two structures were contemporaneous, but in the period running up to the Clearances in the early 1800s, there was often increasing pressure on the land due to a rising population, meaning that shieling grounds were often adapted to become permanent residences with larger, more enduring stone structures, and this may well have been one such case. Clearly, both structures were pretty ancient, almost certainly pre-clearance and the shieling appeared to be older than the stone building footings.

Pleased with locating the building and finding the shieling, I carried on around the south end of the loch and was presented with

magnificent views down the length of Srath Dionard, with its towering rocky slabs and unstable slopes of scree on either side. I passed
the 3m square concrete base of a former fishing hut (still marked on
the current OS map) and just managed to hop across some boulders
in the Allt an Easain Ghil, not too far up from its outfall into Loch
Dionard, to get to its east bank. This was very convenient, as my
onward route was a hill track rising from the loch's south east end,
disappearing over a high pass way off in the distance, which I had
been observing all the time I was walking around the water's edge.

My usual habit had been to take a drink when I crossed a decent
hill burn, however, as I crossed the Allt an Easain Ghil, what turned
out to be the last burn in the valley, I failed to do this. I think I must
have been keen to press on up the hill and thought I'd encounter more
mountain burns along the way. It was just after 1.00 when I began
the long upward haul and the sun was beating down from above. The
walking was fairly easy on the little-used track, although the gradient
alternated between gentle to some quite steep sections. I stopped
occasionally to admire and take pictures of the stunning scenery (and
take a breath!), as the unfolding vista down Srath Dionard just kept
on getting better and better with height.

Just as spectacular were the views to the south west up the Allt an
Easain Ghil valley across the drumlin fields, like mini, green pyramids
to the backdrop of the dome-topped, 731m high Creagan Meall Horn.
I even took a self-timed photo of myself in front of Srath Dionard, just
making it off the ground and into the picture after setting the camera
up on a rock, still with my heavy backpack on! There was also a glimpse
into Srath Beag to the north, with Loch Eriboll, a sea-loch stretching
off into the distance beyond. This long and deep loch is where huge
battleships, such as the most mighty of them all, HMS Hood, could
safely anchor during World War II and was also where the 33 U-boats
of the German submarine fleet surrendered in 1945 at the end of the
same conflict. Incidentally, since my walk, the Cape Wrath minibus

driver, David Hird, has been busy getting another book published on this very subject - The Grey Wolves of Eriboll (ISBN 978-1904445-32-6, £16.99).

My water situation was getting worse; I had finished my water bottle and it was getting hotter! At 2.00, just before the last steep section, I decided I'd better break for lunch and took shelter from my old foe, the easterly wind, in the lee of some peat hags. Almost fully recharged with oatcakes, cheese and chocolate, but no water, I slogged up the final uphill section of the track, which was the steepest part of the whole 3km length up from Loch Dionard. I thought that this steep section, with several hair-pin bends, must be pretty hairy in a 4-wheeled drive vehicle and was quite thankful I had full, albeit slow, control on foot. At the top of the bealach, the track passed within 50m of the summit of what was really a minor hill in these parts, Creag an Staonsaid, standing at 454m high. The vegetation on the top consisted of pale green, short-cropped grass, moss and lichens and was almost tundra-like in appearance, especially with the bare rock slabs littering the surface at these heights.

At the cairn I took in the view. It was just magnificent. Foinaven and Cranstackie stood out proudly to the north and the most northerly Munro in Scotland, Ben Hope, with its whole frontal face carved almost vertically by Ice Age glaciers, lay to the north east. Ben Loyal was in the distance to the east and, even further off, were the Ben Griams - Mor and Beg. Ben Hee and Ben Klibreck were prominent in the south east, in the direction I was heading. I felt on top of the world - and thirsty!

The track dropped just as steeply down from the top for the first 2km on the south east side of Creag an Staonsaid, as it led towards the fertile, birch-lined Glen Golly and Gobernuisgach Lodge beyond. There were signs on the track that I was not the first to have passed this way, probably not too recently, given the length of the dry spell we were experiencing at that time; the impressions of mountain bike tyres could be seen in what had at one time been muddy pools, but there were no footprints or vehicle tyre marks.

For the 2½ days I'd been walking by then, I felt very pleased with what I was doing and very at ease with my own little world. I'd made reasonable progress, the weather had been perfect (wind apart, but I'd take that over rain, any day), I'd seen some fantastic sights and stumbled across a whole host of interesting things from archaeology to flora and fauna. I had never been bored for one minute and again I imagined what people would say to me when I got back – '*Ooh, but weren't you bored?*' How could I possibly have been bored?!! Almost every minute, the scene changed; almost every minute, there was something new to see; and almost every minute, there was something to find and investigate, if you were of an inquisitive persuasion. I admit that it would have been completely different if it was lashing with rain the whole time and, if this *had* been the case, I may well have called it a day. It would have been absolutely miserable! I never relish the prospect of trudging through bogs in the wet, in soaking clothing and sleeping in a damp tent. That's no fun at all to me, and I wasn't doing this just to get directly from A to B. I was enjoying the whole, all round experience in pleasant weather, with no beasties and low vegetation. This trip had already been one of the best things I'd ever done and there was more, much more still to come. I was having an absolute ball!

The walking continued to be pretty easy on this stony track, but the steep downhill sections didn't do much for my burgeoning blisters. I knew it wouldn't be too far before I crossed a burn to satisfy my raging thirst, but the first one marked on the map had dried up completely during this recent arid spell! I eventually got my relieving drink from the Allt Beith a' Mheadhoin, as the track crossed on a wooden bridge at the head of Glen Golly, around 5km and 2½ hours (including my dry lunch stop) since I'd finished the water in my bottle.

Suitably refreshed, I walked on along the flat-bottomed valley floor to where it suddenly and dramatically opened into a deep gully, with the beautiful Easan Choineas waterfall dropping 20m or so from its far side, around 100m further down from the head of the ravine. It was odd, looking upstream from the waterfall, seeing an empty gorge where a waterfall had once flowed over its leading edge. The Glen Golly River had obviously formed the whole extent of this great cre-vasse in the valley floor long ago, but its course had cut down through softer sediments over time, diverting it away from the rocky head of the gorge it had originally incised, to flow in further down from its side. With the sun still shining brightly and blue skies all around, the rushing white curtain of water falling into a great, menacingly dark plunge-pool below, all surrounded by spring-green birch trees, moss and heather hugging the grey rocky cliffs of the gorge, all made for another magnificent and majestic sight.

Somewhere across the other side in the scattered birch trees, I could hear a male cuckoo doing what it does, calling for a female mate. I hadn't seen much bird-life today, apart from the omnipresent skylark, and it was a refreshing change to hear the sound of a different bird, as I fell into a flat-bottomed, but quite narrow, steep-sided part of Glen Golly. In places along the track before the level, small burns rushing down from the side had partly washed away the track, so that it would probably not even have been passable now by a 4-wheeled drive vehicle. On the flat, I noticed that the cuckoo's birch trees, which clung to the steep far side of the glen, looked a bit odd, as many of the trunks grew perpendicularly out of the ground for a few metres before turning normally to grow upright. It looked as if the whole glen side had been tilted about 45^0.

The valley gradient had tailed off to almost level and there was a lush strip of grass growing across the valley floor, at this point around 100m or so wide, then the glen narrowed again as the river fell into another gorge, around ½km downstream. The grassy area was an obvious place for former habitation and I didn't have to look far, as the track led me to where it had actually cut through a shieling, almost completely obliterating it and another two were left unscathed between it and the river. These, again, were 'new' shielings, which had not been previously recorded on the HER, so, as it was 4.45 and I had only made 12km today, I quickly set about recording their position and describing them. I later discovered that there *were* two small buildings in this area depicted on the OS 1st edition map, and these were evidently the shielings, but they had not been observed by the RCAHMS or recorded on the HER.

Set on the raised grassy area on this river terrace, the main shieling was another lozenge-shaped dwelling, measuring 3m x 5m externally, and the smaller one nearby was circular in shape, with an external diameter of 3m. The moss-covered stone walls of the lozenge shieling had collapsed to around 1m wide and were standing around 0.6m high, and its 0.6m wide entrance was placed centrally on its long south east side. Its reedy interior was the narrowest I'd yet seen, measuring only 1.7m x 3.6m. The nearby circular shieling, 10m to the south, had an internal diameter of only 1.5m, with its grassy peat walls being 0.7m in width and only around 0.25m high. It had a narrow, 0.3m wide entrance on its north side, facing towards the main shieling. The larger structure was probably living accommodation for the shieling dwellers, as was the one destroyed when the track was built and the smaller, circular shieling was probably used for storing supplies.

Pleased with this new find, I set off again down the track, which rose up high above the valley floor as the river passed into the narrow, impassable gorge. On top of the higher ground, I could see in the distance a few kilometres to the south, the next estate track which was to be my route winding gently up a slope below the huge, almost flat-ended north east ridge of Beinn Direach.

Gobernuisgach Lodge also came into sight, with its oasis of manicured grass, contrasting to the comparatively barren wild lands surrounding it. Not too much earlier, I had been thinking that I hadn't seen even a single deer today on the hills. Would you believe it - when

I got closer to the lodge, I could see that the well kept grass was being kept well by around a dozen of the beasts! It was just so ironic; I had walked 15km without seeing a single deer on the wild hills, then on passing the only civilisation for miles around, the place was almost bristling with them! Three or four were just lying down, taking in the last rays of the evening spring sunshine, whilst the rest were grazing contentedly on the lawns and all were aware of my presence, even though I was still around 500m away. It appeared as if no-one else was home, but I could hear the generator working away, so the lodge was certainly in use.

The impressive 2-storyed lodge was built in 1845 and it stood at the river's edge facing north west up Glen Golly. It is described by Elizabeth Beaton in her 'Sutherland: an Illustrated Architectural Guide' (1995) as *a simple gabled, shallow U-plan house*, and there was a keeper's house set back from the lodge to its south east. Some outbuildings, including a deer larder and a byre completed the complex. The whole lodge setting was so neat; the five grey stone buildings, flashed with the black and white colours of the super-wealthy Westminster Estate, a small, bright white picket fence, a few pine trees and the beautiful deep green grass all combined to make it a very pretty sight. Incidentally, the corporate estate colours apply to almost everything within the estate boundaries; the British Telecom telephone box at Achfary, around 10km to the south east of Laxford Bridge on the A838, is an example of this, as it, too, is painted black and white!

It was just before 6.00 when the track I was on terminated at a T junction with another, which led from the lodge, via the Bealach nam Meirleach, to the A838 at West Merkland. I turned right onto this track, heading away from the lodge, as I was going to follow it for around 3km uphill, before veering off cross country to what I'd earmarked as my night's resting place: the shores of Loch a' Choire Leacaich, still 7km away.

The pleasant evening sunshine continued as I marched uphill on this well-maintained track. The height I was gaining enabled me to see again the high hills all around, which had previously disappeared from my view when I was in the lower reaches of Glen Golly. I welcomed back Ben Hope and Ben Loyal and reacquainted myself with the impressive massif of Beinn Direach (living up to its translated name of the Upright/Ascending Mountain), to which I was getting ever closer. As I passed the elongate coire which led directly to beneath the Beinn and the crags below the ridge's abrupt north east end, a few underprivileged cousins of the deer who were living a luxurious lifestyle at Gobernuisgach were foraging for a less nutritious existence at this height. Around 1.5km along this section of track, I passed another quite significant psychological point – I had crossed onto the next OS Landranger Map; I was now on Sheet 16 (Lairg, Loch Shin) and no longer needed Sheet 9 (Cape Wrath), which had served me well from the start to here.

As the track levelled out, I gingerly crossed the Allt a' Chraois (Wide Mouthed River) on some conveniently placed boulders, and set off once more on the soft underfoot conditions of the moorland. It was such a pleasant change, as I had spent the whole day, apart from the section along the side of Loch Dionard earlier that morning, on hard estate tracks. This had made for fairly good progress in terms of distance covered, but had been pretty tough on my hard-pummelled feet. The rise out of the Allt a' Chraois valley was fairly gentle and, crossing the shoulder of the lower slopes at the extreme north east end of Ben Hee, I left the parish of Durness behind for good, crossing over the parish boundary into Farr. From here, a new scene came into view over the foreground of Loch Coire na Saidhe Duibhe (Coire Loch of the Black Hay); Ben Klibreck, the south end of which I would be crossing, hopefully, the next day, was not too far off in the evening sunlight and the Ben Griams reappeared, with Caithness beyond.

In the shelter of the Ben Hee massif, the wind had dropped and the sun had disappeared, as I began to negotiate the steep, craggy slopes of the west side of the loch. I considered dropping down to the level of the loch and finding a site, as this coire was sheltered from the wind and it was already 8.30. However, as the rocky terrain, largely covered in deep heather with steep slopes right down to the water's edge, didn't really allow for anything suitable, I decided to press on as I thought there would be better sites at my intended destination at Loch a' Choire Leacaich (Coire Loch of the Flagstones). Way above me on the craggy skyline, a solitary deer peered over the top wondering what was invading its privacy, before needlessly disappearing from view thinking it was under threat.

The going on the steep sides was a bit tricky, on what had been up till then a relatively easy day's walking. There was much clambering to be done on some rocky slabs and the softer terrain was incredibly uneven and not at all helped by deep, leg-catching heather. Ahead of me, more deer were keeping watchful eyes on me, eventually breaking into a panicky run all the way up the bealach I was heading towards myself. They then observed me warily from the top, silhouetted just like the Red Indians in all those 'Westerns' before the wagon-train is slaughtered, prior to disappearing completely as I slowly made my way diagonally uphill.

On the higher ground over the last few hundred metres, the going improved and, as the slope levelled out, I could see an estate track below me passing the east side of the Loch Coire na Saidhe Duibhe. This led all the way across 8km of open, barren and desolate moorland to the Hope road, west of Mudale.

I was soon on the top of the bealach (no sign of the deer) and the steep rocky terrain had given way to grassy peat hags. My stay in the parish of Farr had been brief, for the bealach marked the parish boundary with Lairg, into which I then passed. The down side to being at this spot was that I was no longer in the shelter of the wind and it was blowing quite fiercely at this height of 400m. As I walked across the peat hags towards the loch around 500m away, I could hardly believe the sight at the loch's far end; there was what looked like one of those large, green agricultural buildings found on farms and crofts and it was just *enormous*. My eyes were streaming with the wind blowing hard in my face and, when I had cleared them, I could then see that the 'building' was actually a perfectly rectangular rock the size of a large house, which had fallen from the steep east crags of Ben Hee. It was quite a sight and I did get a bit of a shock, thinking that the estate had been busy constructing a very remote, small industrial complex!

I walked across the undulating peat hags, relieved that I was close to my day's journey end, but the loch surrounds didn't look as though they were going to provide me with a good site to camp, so I had the bright idea of camping in the shelter of one of the deep peat hags. The peat was perfectly dry in most places, so I selected a pretty flat bit and set up camp there (Plate 9), out of the, by now, bitterly cold, evening wind at 9.30. The pegs which were holding down my guy ropes were not very secure as there was no purchase in the dry peat, but the tent was largely out of the wind and I thought it would hold quite comfortably. I wasn't changing my site now at this time of almost 10.00!

Where the tent was pitched was quite a way from the loch, so I took my water from a peaty lochan closer to the tent. The water was fine, but very dark and it had tiny flecks of black peat in it for good measure. I cooked my meal and reflected on the glorious day I'd just had. I was camping at another spectacular site, which had the towering rocky crags of Ben Hee, with heather-covered scree cones at their base, to my west, the beautiful loch to my south and the long moorland slope up to the summit of Creag Dubh Mhor to my south east. What more could I possibly want?

Snuggled up in my sleeping bag after eating my pasta, I pored over the map plotting tomorrow's route, somewhere during which would take me past the half-way point in my trip. I looked over the country covered today and calculated I'd walked around 23km and I felt pretty pleased with my progress. I wrote up my diary of the day's events, then turned out my light at 11.30, my latest night yet.

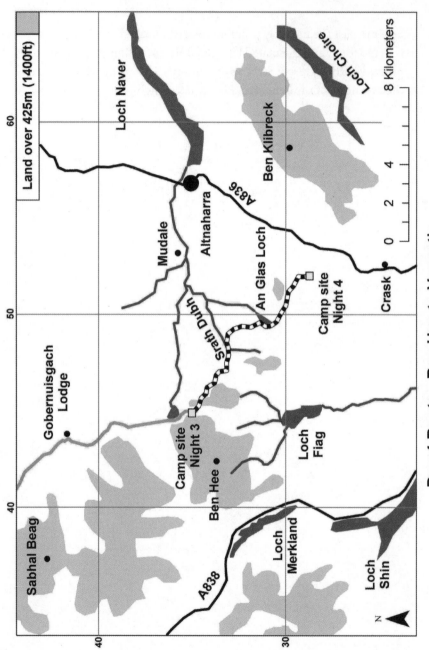

Day 4 Route - Ben Hee to Vagastie

6

DAY 4: BEN HEE TO VAGASTIE

The bright sun was shining again against a background of radiant blue skies, when I zipped down my tent door at 9.00, and the cool wind was still blowing from the south-east. By 10.30, I'd had my breakfast and everything was packed and ready to go. The one bad thing I found about camping on dry peat was that after walking on it, around the vicinity of the tent, it almost instantly turned to a fine dust, which got everywhere. My hands yesterday had taken a bit of a pasting from the sun and were pretty burnt and red, so with the sun being out again today, I found myself in the ludicrous position of wearing gloves to protect them further from the hot sun!

From my peaty campsite, I rose up the gentle moorland slope to the east, to a small pass between Bad a' Bhacaidh and the 553m high Creag Dhubh Mor. As I gained height, the views back towards my night's resting place became better and better, as more and more of the Ben Hee massif came into view. The mountain absolutely dwarfed my campsite and there were still some patches of snow on its upper slopes. On the slope I was walking up, there were a few small ponds, on which there were those skilful little insects, Pondskaters, marshalling the surface of the water, like general foremen. It's always fascinating to watch these wizards of the water; apparently, as their name implies, skating on the pond, leaving curving depressions on its surface beneath their legs. Below the surface, there were many fat tadpoles, spending their time trying to escape my looming presence by burrowing into the soft, cloudy sediment at the bottom of the pool. Their main problem was not me; it was more of a life or death race against time to see if they would develop and leave the water - before the water left them, by evaporation, during this long, dry spell.

The gentle hill gradient made for fairly easy going at the start of my fourth day. The slope was absolutely littered with loose slabs which had been deposited by melting glaciers at the end of the last Ice Age and there were three much larger boulders (or were they *bone fide* rock outcrops?) stuck into the dry bog, which had been adorned by a few of these smaller slabs, like beacons marking a route. After crossing back into the parish of Farr at the bealach and skirting around the north east flank of Creag Dhubh Mor, I was greeted with another magnificent view, this time across the vast expanse of peat bog to the north and east, to Ben Hope and Ben Loyal far off in the distance. The expanse *was* vast, but not featureless, as there were many small lochans and the Allt Coire na Saidhe Duibhe draining the whole area in the middle distance. Looking through my binoculars, I scanned the plains below and marked on my map some areas of lush green along the river's length which could well be sites for potential archaeology, but which I would definitely *not* be visiting on this trip as they were far, far away, apart from one I'd spotted in a strath ahead of me.

Suddenly, to my right, there was a dart and a flash, which I caught out of the side of my eye. It was a Mountain Hare which was scurrying up the hillside and eventually came to rest around 40m on the slope above me. It stopped on a flat rock slab and sat up on its hind legs, looking uphill, without even glancing back at me. I slowly took out my camera, hoping it wouldn't be disturbed, and snapped it a couple of times. It was still partly in its winter coat, so was actually a dappled

Plate 1 – Day 1 – The Kyle of Durness ferry approaching Keoldale slipway

Plate 2 – Day 1 – Spectacular sea arch & stacks in upright Lewisian Gneiss rocks

Plate 3 – Day 1 – Campsite overlooking Sandwood Bay and Am Buachaille

Plate 4 – Day 2 – Remains of a 9m long Killer Whale on Sandwood Bay beach
(A6 size notebook at mouth for scale)

Plate 5 – Day 2 – The ruin of Balloch, looking west towards Creag Riabhach

Plate 6 – Day 3 – The clear water of Allt Coire na Lurgainn below A' Che'ir Gorm

Plate 7 – Day 3 – Bare rock cliffs of Creag Urbhard towering above Loch Dionard

Plate 8 – Day 3 – A mini-ecosystem on a large boulder at Loch Dionard

*Plate 9 – Day 3 – Campsite in peat hags at the head of Loch a' Choire Leacaich,
below the steep slopes of Ben Hee*

Plate 10 – Day 4 – A lone young stag atop a drumlin in Srath a Dhuibh

Plate 11 – Day 4 – A shieling (marked by rocks and heather) in Srath a Dhuibh (The Sanctury)

Plate 12 – Day 4 – Overlooking 'The Sanctuary', with patches of snow on Ben Hee in the distance

Plate 13 – Day 4 – The ruined farmstead at the head of An Glas-loch, with Ben Loyal in the backgorund

Plate 14 – Day 5 – A huge herd of Red Deer in Srath a' Chraisg
with modern forest plantation in the background

Plate 15 – Day 5 – Overlooking Loch Gaineamhach and the Loch Choire glen beyond

Plate 16 – Day 5 – Buzzed by a jet overlooking the source of the River Brora

Plate 17 – Day 5 – Old pine tree stump in peat in the bank of Allt Gobhlach

Plate 18 – Day 6 – The more common pink and the very rare white Lousewort

Plate 19 – Day 6 – Violet Ground Beetle on Sphagnum Moss

Plate 20 – Day 6 – Otter returning to Allt Gobhlach after scent-marking a boulder

Plate 21 – Day 6 – The view down Upper Strath Brora

Plate 22 – Day 6 – Dreaded ticks 'questing' on the top of a long grass stalk

Plate 23 – Day 7 – Carrol Rock and Loch Brora from the old township of Ledoch

Plate 24 – Day 7 – Journey's end, where the River Brora joins the Moray Firth

white and grey. It sat for a few minutes as I gazed at it, then it took off as if it didn't have a care in the world, and, I guess, it probably didn't. With this great view below me and fresh from my encounter with the hare, I switched my mobile phone on to see if I could get a signal, and sure enough all of the strength bars lit up. I checked in at home and reported my recent sighting to Jacquie, who I sensed was a bit envious, to say the least!

After completing my call, I carried on skirting around the mid level of Creag Dhubh Mor, before dropping down to a small, but prominent gorge incised into the peat on the north side of the Srath a' Dhuibh (Black Valley). I spotted some deer in the distance and searched my bum-bag for my binoculars. They were not there! I searched again, as if by some form of magic they would re-appear after the first search, and they still weren't there this second time; surprise, surprise! I was annoyed with myself, as I must have popped them into the crevice between my bum-bag and my stomach, after I'd used them to admire the view when I was first distracted by the hare. They must have subsequently popped out as I continued walking, without me even noticing, around a kilometre back. I thought that there was little chance of retracing my exact steps to find them, so I accepted my loss, but would miss them over the rest of the trip. So, that was that. Binoculars gone. At least my load would be lighter!

I dropped down into the small gorge, about 5m deep, to get a drink and, as the hot sun shone brightly from above, I was happy to find that it was completely sheltered from the wind there. It was so warm, as it was a real sun-trap, and the water itself was actually not at all cold, as it invariably is in mountain burns, that I decided to wash my hair (what little I had) and stubble. In past experience when I have washed my hair in mountain burns, the ice-cold water really, physically hurts your head, but this was *just* idyllic. It was almost like having a lukewarm outdoor shower, under the intense heat of the midday sun. Almost Mediterranean!

Suitably refreshed in all departments, I continued downstream, sheltered from the wind at the side of the gorge and immediately spied what looked like a solitary black stag on the far side of the valley. No binoculars! I was still able to get a close up, however, as I improvised and took a digital photograph of it and magnified it on the rear screen. Oh, the wonders of modern technology! It was, indeed, almost black, as it must have been wallowing in a muddy peat hag somewhere. Deer frequently indulge in this behaviour, probably as a way of ridding themselves of pests, such as ticks (which, thankfully, I hadn't seen at all yet), and the coating of peat probably also makes a good barrier against midges, which also fortunately weren't actually around yet. Perhaps they do it for none of these reasons. Perhaps they just like it!

Once I had emerged from the bottom of the gorge, my route now took me along the north side of the Allt an Srath a' Dhuibh, known locally on the Altnaharra Estate as 'The Sanctuary'. The flat bottomed valley floor was spiked, further down, with several drumlins; great cones of debris deposited by glaciers which receded 10,000 years ago. Atop the largest of an adjacent pair of these, which rose to 10m high in the centre of the glen, stood a young stag (Plate 10). For all intents and purposes, he was playing 'King of the Castle' with his three other pals below him, beside the river. When they realised there was 'danger' approaching, they made a rapid retreat further down the valley, not waiting to see if I was going to challenge their altitude supremacy, which, actually, I had not the slightest intention of doing!

It was just after 1.00 when I crossed to the south side of the river, to the grassy area I spotted when I last used my recently departed binoculars, around 2km away. I was sure it would be a suitable site for shielings, at least, and it didn't take me long to home in on my first archaeology of the day. One beautiful, lozenge-shaped shieling (Plate 11), measuring 6.5m x 3m, was set lengthways down the gentle slope of a grass-covered alluvial fan, formed from a side burn running into the main Allt an Srath a' Dhuibh. The shieling walls comprised a single course of partly moss-covered boulders and the eastern side was covered in heather. Its entrance was centrally placed in the eastern longwall, which stood around 0.3m high and was spread up to 1m in width. The interior was positively spacious, measuring 1.8m x 5m. There were another possible two shielings close by; a lozenge-shaped one, 16m to its north east and a circular one 10m to the east, but these were not as striking as the main dwelling at this serenely beautiful, peaceful location.

It was 1.45 when I'd finished with the un-named shieling settlement; its name had must have been lost over the centuries after it went out of use, probably as a direct result of the Clearances. I wasn't even sure where the folk who used these shieling grounds lived permanently, although it was probably the old cleared township of Tumore, some 5km to the east. I pressed on up the valley side slope, making my way towards the ridge over the shoulder coming from the north east side of Meall an Amairich. When I had gained plenty of height, I rewarded myself with lunch at 2.00, overlooking, from an altitude of 320m, the majestic sight of the long 'Sanctuary' valley, with its meandering ribbon of a river stretching out way below me (Plate 12), drumlins popping out all over the place - and it was *still* hot and sunny!

After taking in the scenery and my cheese, oatcake and melting chocolate lunch, I set off towards the crest of the ridge and my next vista appeared. To the north east, looking into the distance along the ridge, there were small, neatly ordered, dark green parcels of pine forestry, in regularly spaced plantations in a horizontal line along the Hope road to Altnaharra. To the east was the massive whaleback form of the 961m Munro, Ben Klibreck, with a whole new swathe of moorland in front of the valley of Allt a' Ghlas-locha (River of the Grey Loch). The moorland stretched away for 1.5km below me, before it reached the river, which was not actually visible itself, as it had cut a deep channel through the peat and lay below the general ground level. There were many deer, like brown dots on a huge piece of beige paper, grazing on this expanse below me and it was as though I had my own wildlife park through which to roam.

There were occasional grassy patches attached to the banks of this distant river, flowing north from An Glas-loch (the Grey Loch) to join the River Mudale, which I thought would be rife for archaeology. However, I was not travelling in that direction and would have to leave that valley for another time. I was heading for some archaeology which *was* known (a building, HER Ref: MHG18675, observed by the RCAHMS from the OS map) at the south end of the loch. Looking towards this area, I could see what I thought was a patch of dark reeds in the loch, where its feeder river, Allt Preas Braigh nan Allt, flowed in. I also spotted one good green patch, directly below my vantage point, on the north western shore of the loch, which I thought would be worthy of investigation; a minor diversion to this part of the loch was worth the gamble in the quest for new archaeology, after all! I made for a small burn flowing from below me to the south east, which had also incised itself into the peat, as it made its way down the moderate south east slopes of Meall an Amairich into An Glas-loch.

Wouldn't you know it? The wee detour paid off. Not only did I get some arty photographic shots of a lone, forlorn-looking rowan tree in the small gorge, with the entire khaki-speckled crest of Meall an Fhuarain in the background, but on arriving at the green patch on the shore, there was, indeed, some archaeology as predicted! It was a lovely, lozenge-shaped shieling, with a distinctive central Sutherland architectural feature of a circular, blister-like bulge from the side of its upper end. In plan, it was almost like a skewed figure-of-eight and I had seen this design before, from my previous long jaunt three years earlier, at a site east of Loch Coire Lodge, 17km exactly due east of here. On closer inspection, it was even more of a complex design than I'd first thought, as there was the faint outline of a rectangular 'annexe' constructed on its south west side, running the full length of the shieling.

Set with its longsides parallel to the gentle gradient of the grassy, alluvial fan, created by the un-named burn I'd followed down to the shore of An Glas-loch, this unusual shaped dwelling was 20m from the water's edge. The remains of its single coursed wall of boulders, standing up to 0.4m high and 0.5m wide, clearly depicted its outline, which measured 4.5m x 2.5m externally, leaving only 3m x 1.4m of internal space. The north east 'cell' was slightly oval, measuring 2.5m x 2m externally and was connected internally to the main lozenge by a 0.6m wide doorway. The angular-cornered annexe, attached to the south west side of the main part of the shieling, appeared to be a later addition and was also connected to it by an internal doorway. An interesting design and adaptation to add to the collection, I thought, after I'd recorded the previously unknown structural complex, and I set off again at 3.50, able to walk on the exposed stony loch shore due to its low water level.

As I ambled along the shoreline, I passed a mass of feathers in the heather, where a snipe had come to a sad end at the hands, or rather the claws, of a large bird of prey or, perhaps, a fox. I also noticed that the 'reeds' I'd observed earlier, from the high vantage point over a kilometre away, had mysteriously disappeared and a single stag was up to its belly in the water at the same location. It dawned on me that the 'reeds' had been, in fact, a herd of deer, probably all stags, which were cooling off in the heat of the sun. Most of the paddling deer had fled the vulnerability of the loch for the safety of the land, leaving this one fearless beast all alone in the water.

By the time I reached the head of the loch, the stag had disappeared and I crossed to the east bank of the shallow-running Allt Preas Braigh nan Allt fairly easily, on convenient stones, to home in on the building recorded on the HER. It was not difficult to locate; its stone walls stood 0.7m high and formed a small rectangular outline, and it was perched on the bank around 10m above the main river and next to a small tributary (Plate 13). The building remains were orientated NW-SE, with its north west gable end facing the river and it measured only 7m x 4m. It was divided into two small, equal sized compartments by a central wall with a connecting doorway between, and the entrance to the whole building was at the river end of the building's north east side. The double-skinned boulder walls still comprised 4 or 5 courses in most places and were around 0.9m thick. It was a diminutive, isolated building which would have supported a small family and was situated miles away from the nearest permanent settlement.

Pleased with the first recording of this previously unvisited site, I left at 5.00, only to find a shieling on the grassy area around 80m to its north east, across another small tributary of the main river. This discovery was not entirely unexpected, as I had seen the large grassy area it occupied from afar, and had been making for it to explore after I had located the stone building I'd just recorded. However, after coming across this one shieling, I spotted another, then another and another and another. In all, there was the incredible total of *twelve* shielings of four different designs on this gently north west-sloping alluvial fan, which had been created by the tributary of the Allt Preas Braigh nan Allt. There were 6 of the lozenge shape, 3 figure-of-eights, two circular ones and a U-shaped shieling, and these would have supported a large thriving summer community of women, children and their livestock. Their parent township was possibly Mudale and maybe the stone building and the shieling co-existed side-by-side for a few decades.

This site certainly would have been a place full of activity during the summer months. In fact, I reckoned that if I had been doing this walk 200 years or more ago, I'd have been amongst throngs of people for much of the entire trip. I had seen absolutely no-one on my trek so far, but I genuinely wouldn't have been able to escape the bustle of people engaged in shieling life in those times if I'd been here a couple of centuries previously. The land would have been buzzing with folk engaged in their daily activities of herding their livestock on the hills, hunting for their food on the lochs and rivers, spinning wool and occupying all of the shieling dwellings I'd discovered. What a change had been brought about by the Clearances, with the glens and straths no longer echoing to the sounds of their summer visitors and, in some cases, their permanent inhabitants. Oh, to have been there then; I would have gladly sacrificed my delightful solitude at that moment, just to get a glimpse of what it was like in those distant and so different days.

By finding all of these shielings, my progress for the rest of the day was going to be severely hindered. I wanted to record the position and description of each one, as it was pretty likely that I would never return here again. It was 6.20 before I was able to leave the site after completing my recording 'duties', to begin the trudge up and over the 380m high final ridge of the day, the south west shoulder of Meall an Fhuarain.

I had, by now, given up hope of crossing the A836 today, and so was aiming to camp somewhere on the ridge's south east side. As I rose up the slope beside the tributary, I began to see again the extent of the shieling grounds of An Glas-loch spreading out below me. It was very clear that the grassy alluvial fan, on which the shielings were situated, had been formed by deposits carried by the tributary as it had incised through the thick peat and glacial sediment, leaving a deep scar on the hillside. The fan provided again, a lush, light green oasis on the valley floor, compared to the remainder of the darker green and brown of the heather-clad valley sides.

I disturbed a herd of around 30 Red Deer on the way up the slope and they retreated over the skyline as I plodded on in their direction. On top of the ridge, the cold wind bit hard again. New scenery behind me to the south-west compensated a little for this, as it unfolded into view. Layers of landscapes, fading in colour with increasing distance in the evening atmosphere, passed towards the backdrop of the mountain range dominated by the 998m high Ben More Assynt. Still lingering in its high, north-facing corries, were large white patches of snow and its rugged, serrated ridge provided the distant termination of this spectacular mountainous panorama. In my onward direction to the east, across some dark, peaty lochans, Ben Klibreck rose gloriously in the evening sunshine, backed by clear, pale-blue skies. The lochans were filled with Cotton Grass, reeds and Sphagnum Moss and, with their water levels low at this time, many had jet black 'beaches' of soft peat at the water's edge, in stark contrast to the deep blue of the water reflecting the high, early summer sky. This was the ultimate Freeview, on the widest of widescreen TVs!

From this vantage point, I also had my first glimpse of the A836, the lifeline road connecting Lairg, in the centre of Sutherland with Tongue, on its north coast. The single track 'A' class road rises up gently from Vagastie to the south, past the pine shelter belt which protects it from drifting snow in winter time. At 266m above sea level, this is the highest public road in Sutherland, just north of the Crask Inn; a very lonely, but welcoming outpost to the traveller, some 5km away to my south.

Once over the boggy, lochan-strewn, broad-topped ridge, I picked a route down an un-named burn, which met two others at a small grassy spot at the head of a valley, to form the Allt Bealach an Fhuarain. I decide to make for this, as it looked a possible location for a shieling and earmarked another, around 1km lower down the main burn, which looked larger and, therefore, even more promising. It didn't take me too long to get down this slope to the first area where the burns met, however, it was too small to yield anything archaeological, so I carried on due south following the amalgamated water of the three burns. At 8.00, I came to a small, grassy river terrace on a bend, which was below the general ground level of the valley. It was fairly sheltered from the wind and, as there looked to be few other such sheltered places within easy reach downstream, I decided to call it a day there and leave the next patch of green for tomorrow.

While I was getting my tent ready, I spotted the first tick of the trip which had crawled onto my rucksack while it was lying on the ground, and saw several more on this small patch of grass, which didn't please me. I had the tent up by 8.30 and was cooking my pasta meal in the fading evening sunshine. Another reason for not continuing on that evening was that I wanted to stop before the sun finally set over the hills, as sitting, eating your meal in the last of the sun's rays is just lovely – I had been walking too late to get this effect the previous evening. I had also felt a blister maturing nicely on each foot and that was just as important a factor for my relatively early finish.

Once zipped up in my tent and in my sleeping bag, I pondered over my day and planned my route for tomorrow. Today, I had only covered 9km, as my friend the crow would have flown, and maybe 11km in total walked distance. This was not a day for real progress, but it had again been a day of joy and beauty; the weather had been glorious, I had been thrilled by the scenery, especially in the glen of the Allt an Srath a' Dhuibh, and had discovered much, mainly unrecorded archaeology. It couldn't get better than this ... could it?

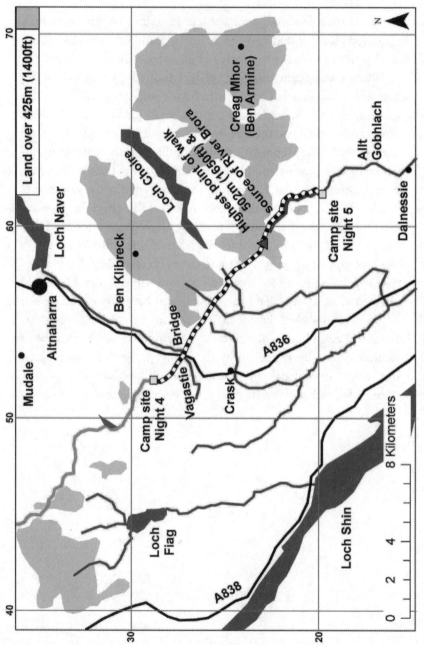

Land over 425m (1400ft)

N

Mudale

Altnaharra

Loch Naver

Ben Klibreck

Loch Choire

Creag Mhor
(Ben Armine)

Highest point of walk
502m (1650ft) &
source of River Brora

Bridge

Vagastie

Crask

A836

Camp site
Night 4

Camp site
Night 5

Allt
Gobhlach

Dalnessie

Loch
Fiag

Loch Shin

A838

0   2   4   8 Kilometers

Day 5 Route - Vagastie to Allt Gobhlach

7

DAY 5: VAGASTIE TO ALLT GOBHLACH

After a good night's sleep, apart from dwelling a little on the unwelcome approach into tick country, I unzipped my tent door at 8.30 to be welcomed again by clear blue skies and sunshine, and a cool south-easterly breeze. After my usual morning preliminaries, I was packed and ready to leave the site by 10.00 and was off down the Allt Bealach an Fhuairain. I hadn't even covered a kilometre when I reached the burn-side grassy area I'd been making for the previous evening and immediately came across unrecorded archaeology. The moss-covered, stone-walled remains of a small (7.5m x 3m) rectangular building, standing around 0.6m high, set 15m from the edge of the west bank of the burn was a very obvious structure. Tucked against the bank of the river terrace, which afforded it protection from the prevailing westerlies and set parallel to the burn, the building was subdivided into two unequal sized compartments, which weren't internally connected and the narrow external doorways both faced out to the water.

On the other, east side of the burn, the grassy area was more extensive and, needless to say, there was more to be found there. Two barrel-shaped (square-ended lozenges) shieling remains were set opposite the stone-walled building, both set at an oblique angle to the burn. I assumed that these shielings, one measuring 7m x 3m and the other 5.5m x 3m, were precursors to the more permanent building across the burn. They were both of a similar design, having two internally connected compartments, the smaller ones both being at their south east ends. The walls of the larger shieling were moss-covered boulders, whereas the smaller one had only a little stonework visible under grass. The walls stood around 0.4m high and 0.6m wide.

A third shieling was situated back on the west bank, around 100m downstream, on level ground only 2m from the river bank's edge. This was quite a substantial structure, larger than any of the other three dwellings recorded just upstream of here. The rectangular remains of the building measured 9m x 3m and it was split into two separate, unconnected compartments, with both doorways facing east, looking out to the river. The more substantial remains of the larger, northern section had stone walls visible, protruding through the grass and moss, whereas the walls of the southern part appeared to be largely, if not all, of turf. Sheltering the northern gable end were the mounded, moss-covered stone remains of an interesting and unusual protecting wall, standing around 0.6m high. So much for the planned early progress today!

This discovery made me very happy (I'm easily pleased!), as, not only had I discovered some more archaeology at a site where I thought there was likely to be some, but if I hadn't stopped at my campsite the previous night, I'd have got bogged down with recording this archaeology and been left with nowhere sheltered to camp at all. Sometimes, it felt as though everything was going just right for me and my, by now, good friend, St Christopher, was still on my side!

Crossing the river just downstream, I was ready to climb the final ridge before the A836, more or less marking the central part between the west and east coasts. A solitary bright yellow flower growing on the shingle shore of a bend in the river caught my eye. It was sharing its situation with several other hardy Common Dog-violet flowers, but I was very surprised to discover that it was no more than a common Dandelion, which had lodged itself on this barren ground and had obviously taken firm root. I thought that cultivated ground was the favoured site of the weed, but this seed from a clock must have been carried on the wind from such an area to here, and had taken root many miles from the nearest population.

From the burn to the south shoulder of Beinn na Glas-choille was only half a kilometre of gentle, uphill walking over tinder-dry grass and lichen, and a view down into Strath Vagastie now appeared ahead of me. It was a gentle amble down the other side towards the Vagastie River, with splendid views of Ben Klibreck beyond. The white cottage of Vagastie and its green sward was in the middle distance, but the whole view was slightly marred by the forest fence enclosing a young pine plantation in the foreground. When I was around 500m from Vagastie Bridge, I saw my first living soul on land since my trek began – a cyclist, puffing in the blistering sunshine as he propelled himself up the gradient on the A836 towards the Crask. I'm sure he didn't see me, and I didn't particularly want to see him, through no fault of his own, I hasten to add; it was just that I was enjoying my own self-imposed solitary confinement. Up till then it had just been me - and the wild!

I took a drink from the river and crossed it, then up the bank to the tarmac of the main arterial road through Central Sutherland. I had driven along this road a hundred times and had even walked across it before at this spot, when I parked my car here one sunny August day in 2002. That day, I was heading for the top of the 961m high Ben Klibreck, but I never thought, whenever I had been here before, that so much euphoria would be associated with merely crossing this road at some time in the future! It was a significant landmark in my journey; it was the real half-way point, yet it was 12.00 on Day 5, with only 2 and a half days left on my schedule to complete my journey!

From the shoulder I had just come down, I had taken note of a further green patch to visit on the east side of Strath Vagastie, where the ribbon burns on the south west flank of the massive heathery dome of Cnoc Sgriodain began. I saw plenty of Cotton Grass, which always indicates that the ground from which it grows is boggy. Its white fluffy cotton bud on the end of a green stalk is readily recognisable, but the message given out by this early summer flowering plant during this current dry spell was very confusing!

Rising up one of the minor burns towards the lofty grassy patch, I came across a small area of grass, on which, almost needless to say, I found a shieling. It was the smallest piece of grazing you could imagine and scarcely sufficient, I thought, to sustain *any* livestock. However, sustain livestock it must have done, as the remains of the structure was proof to tell. It was a square-ended lozenge type, set on the north bank of a small trickle of a burn, and marked by clumps of reeds growing in its interior. Its walls were largely moss-covered mounds, with some stone visible, standing around 0.3m high and 0.7m wide and the whole shieling measured only 4m x 2.5m.

Pressing on up the steepening moorland slope, suddenly at my green target there was a blaze of colour; the lush grassy patch was carpeted in 2 different types of golden yellow flower, Marsh Marigolds and the smaller Lesser Celandines, making the whole area resemble an Alpine meadow. The gradient here, after all, was too steep for any human habitation, but this rich patch must have been used as grazing, more than likely by the occupants of the shieling, some 300m below.

Above this high meadow, the terrain returned to the usual longer grass, lichens and moss. I scared a lone Grouse from its grazing in a clump of heather and, as it took flight, squawking madly and furiously as it escaped, it reciprocally scared the living daylights out of me too! I had seen several piles of grouse droppings on the trip up to this point, each pile consisting of a stack of pale brown, mini-cylindrical, Weetabix-textured extrusions, topped with a flash of white, but it was only the 4th actual grouse I'd seen on the entire excursion so far. It just emphasised to me how much of a decline the species had suffered, even in the last 25 or so years. Grouse were so commonplace in the Highlands at one time, that the landed gentry and their friends, on and after the 'Glorious 12th' (of August), would bag hundreds and hundreds of birds in one shoot. The decline of the grouse must be down in part to this over-zealous pastime of the rich and privileged, and also, apparently, to the general global warming scenario, whereby they are more at risk from pests and parasites. I have also heard local shepherds and gamekeepers talk of a massive rise in the parasite population, especially ticks, from the lack of dipping of sheep. There are also far fewer sheep on the hills these days, so the ticks must have to concentrate on what is there and the grouse, unfortunately for them, would fall into this category.

A 2km trudge over this featureless moorland at the foot of Cnoc Sgriodain, led me to cross from the parish of Farr into the parish of Lairg, before my next planned archaeological site. When on a solitary trip like this, walking over barren landscapes for kilometre after kilometre, or plodding up and over high passes, it's funny what you learn about yourself. I am not a religious person at all (even allowing for previous references to St Christopher!), but, during these times when a distant or high target had to be achieved or the long haul in front appeared to be never ending, I found myself singing or humming hymns and carols in my mind to the pace of my walking. The only reason I could fathom for this is that these religious tunes, such as 'Morning Has Broken', 'O Come All Ye Faithful' and 'Love Divine, All Loves Excelling', all have a rhythm which has the same tempo as my stride. In playing these tunes in my mind, some of the less interesting or more gruelling parts of my walk became more pleasant or more easily achieved. It wasn't something I consciously thought about doing, it just seemed to happen, which I thought was very interesting, if not a little odd!

The new views opening up to the south and east were wide and less rugged and, in truth, a little saddening to me. Draped over the sides and tops of many of the hills were many square kilometres of forestry plantation, a scourge, in my opinion, of the land of the north. In general, you cannot walk through them as they are so dense, so you have to traverse around them - and some are particularly extensive. Should you be able to find any open firebreaks and choose to navigate through, the ground vegetation grows un-naturally long and completely unchecked because grazing wildlife is excluded by the high perimeter fencing and the walking is extremely difficult and uncomfortable, and really not even worth the trouble. Much archaeology within the plantations has certainly been lost in the past, due to unrestricted planting of the trees, before there was a check on this and surveys were required to be undertaken. This, at least in theory, ensures that small, tree-exclusion buffer zones are created around those remains which are discovered.

These softwood pine plantations were a well-known tax dodge in the 1980s and great swathes, of especially Sutherland and neighbouring Caithness, were planted for no other reason than this. The chickens have now come home well and truly to roost and the timber is extremely expensive to fell and extract. The infrastructure cannot readily cope with the volume which has to be hauled to the pulp mills, leaving little, if any, financial reward in the whole process. Up until very recently, estates would have actually made a loss if they had extracted the timber, so the majority of the plantations, especially those in the more remote areas, and therefore the most expensive to fell and extract, have just been left. Several storms in recent years have ripped through these over-mature forests and blown down great swathes of timber as though they were mere matchsticks, making the timber completely worthless if left as wind-blow. When felling ever does take place, the former open moorland or hillside cannot *ever* be restored and is left as a permanent, brashy wasteland, completely un-navigable for walking and unsightly for decades, until natural regeneration or replantation takes hold.

Dismounting now from my high horse and continuing with the account of the journey, I passed over the crest of the high moorland plateau and waved farewell to the view to Ben Loyal and the north, as it began to become obscured from my view by the Ben Klibreck massif in the foreground. The areas of this bog which were usually saturated and squelchy, had currently become completely dried up, and had been left with a silky-smooth purple crust above a slightly soft, peaty substrate beneath. Where deer had walked before me, they had left perfect hoof-prints on this ground and I was doing the same, following, as I was, in their hoof-steps.

Frequently, over the whole trip, my humming march would be interrupted by something on the ground or in the air. Often it was a plant, or an insect, or the usual skylarks. On this occasion, however, at the south west end of the Ben Klibreck range, I was stopped by the sight of a herd of, what must have been upwards of 150 Red Deer, grazing on the fresh, late spring moorland shoots on the wide expanse of Srath a' Chraisg (Plate 14). It was just like the scenes of the wildebeest on the Plains of the Serengeti in a David Attenborough documentary, except it was live and in the flesh, and it was all in front of *just* me. Even if it wasn't quite Africa, it was made that little bit more authentic as the sun beat down onto the wide-rimmed hat I was wearing!

The herd were a good 500m to 1km away and they had become alerted of my presence, even with me being downwind of them. Their eyesight is so keen in spotting something moving or appearing over the horizon and they quickly get spooked and move off, en masse. If you stay still after they have spotted you, then they seem to be ok with this, although they keep a watchful eye on the new statue in their territory. As I continued advancing on them, their retreat was no exception and they were soon on the move, even though I was no threat to them whatsoever. Maybe they have become so timid from centuries of being stalked by hunters, who can pick them off these days with high-powered rifles from hundreds of metres away. This is very different from times well past, when they were chased by man and funnelled into pre-set traps and slaughtered at close range when cornered.

Continuing on towards where the deer had just vacated, I came across a few sink holes, where former streams and those which would form in flash-floods nowadays, would disappear from the land surface to flow through underground channels in the thick blanket of peat. These had been carved by the action of the water over the centuries and there must be a complex, probably interconnecting, system deep below. The largest sink hole was big enough to crawl into on hands and knees and was around 2m beneath the land surface, but I didn't investigate any further by this method at all!

I reached the wide, green grassy channel of the Allt Domhain, which, with its tributaries, drains the whole of the south west end of the Ben Klibreck range. I heard a lone cuckoo, which had colonised a small area of birch trees in one of its tributaries, calling hopefully to a mate and I couldn't help thinking that the bird's task was a bit forlorn, given the nature of the scantily vegetated terrain. I scanned the lush, grassy terraces of the river for any sign of archaeology and continued my search upstream to where it narrowed to a gorge. I was surprised that I could discover nothing archaeological, but remained convinced that this area would have been well used for grazing by shieling dwellers, but their domiciles must have been further downstream. I decided to leave the searching for another, much later day and had lunch at a small cairn on the banks of the small river at 1.45.

While chomping away at my usual lunch of oatcakes and cheese, I caught sight of the silhouette of a large bird, circling high above the peak of Creag an Lochain, part of the Klibreck range, to the north east. There was no doubt that this was a Golden Eagle, Britain's largest and most reclusive bird of prey. It was not the first time I had seen a 'Goldie' on Ben Klibreck, as I was lucky enough to get a really close sighting while on the top during my outing in 2002. This current view was nowhere near as good as that 6 years previously, but I was happy that I'd managed to get a glimpse again this time and add it to my increasing list of wildlife sightings for this trip.

Lunch over; I continued south-eastwards to my next destination, where some archaeology *had* been recorded on the HER. The route skirted the low shoulder on the south east side of the Allt Domhain and I irritated the same large herd of deer I'd disturbed earlier, by marching in their direction again. They dispersed, as before, and I dropped down into the next glen of Allt Doir' a' Bheathaich, to a slightly tumbled, 12m diameter, circular sheepfold, shown on the OS 2nd edition map of 1906, but not recorded on the 1st edition map of 1878. This glen has an old estate track, similarly making its first appearance on the map of 1906, connecting the Crask, to the west, on what is now the A836, with Loch Coire Lodge, to the north east. Uphill from the sheepfold, the track makes a spectacular ascent up to the Bealach Easach, before dropping down into the narrow and deep valley which holds Loch a' Bhealaich and Loch Choire beyond, and is now quite popular with mountain bikers.

Recorded on the HER (Ref No: MHG11576) as a 'Deserted Settlement' and located on the moderate slopes of the opposite, south east side of the valley, my next task was to find it! The area was open and grassy, but there was no obvious sign of any archaeology as I looked across from the sheepfold. No stone, no upstanding remains, just plain, short-cropped, grass-covered slopes on each side of three small burns, separated by areas of heather on slightly more raised ground in between. I really didn't have time to investigate all of the suspect areas, so I homed in on the central green swathe, which was being grazed by a handful of sheep.

After taking a drink and replenishing my water bottle in the main burn, I walked up the valley side searching for the settlement. Right where the grid reference stated, the enigmatic outlines of several small former buildings began to appear. In all, there were five building remains all within around 40m of each other, set with their longsides parallel to the slope and the small burn. They were all of a similar size, approximately 11 or 12m x 3m, although two had outshots (small, original designed jut-outs from the main building line, which were probably used as larders or for a box bed). The subtle wall remains stood barely 0.3m high and were around 0.6m wide and very little stone was visible in their make up; the structures were mostly defined by grassy clumps, sparse reeds and moss.

So there *was* a township here on these north west-facing slopes and the inhabitants must have eked out no more than a subsistence existence at this location, at an altitude of around 320m (1050 feet). On the afternoon I was there, the small burn around which this community was situated was dry, and this was only late spring. It was a good 200-300m walk downhill to reach the more permanent water supply on the valley floor. There must have been more buildings in this settlement, as Jill Harden and Jonathan Wordsworth (the archaeologists engaged to survey the area in 1990, in advance of the now adjacent forestry plantation) recorded the presence of a possible kiln also, which I didn't discover on this particular strip of ground.

As I left the site at 4.00 and marched up the next rise, I took note of the beautiful small, ground-hugging carpets of young bilberry plants. Their plentiful spring leaves were a fresh, bright green, although some clumps of a slightly different strain were tinged with a reddish hue. They all had tiny, pretty pink bulbous flowers, which would be the precursors to the beautifully sweet, tongue-staining bilberry fruits of the autumn.

I had already crossed 3 uphill sections or shoulders today and this was to be the steepest of them all. I had superb views back towards and over the 'invisible' township and my route of earlier in the day, stretching as far as the dominant sight of Ben Hee in the distance, where I had camped two nights earlier. Close to the top of the slope I was on, I decided to take a slight detour. This was to gain a view down onto and along the massive, geological fault-created split, now occupied by Loch a' Bhealaich and, at its far end, Loch Coire, and delineating the south east side of the Ben Klibreck range. The detour involved a short, but fairly steep, ascent of the 469m high Creag Sgoilteach. Once on the top, I could just get a glimpse of the near loch, but the view to the larger and distant Loch Choire was obscured by the hill in the foreground. The view, however, was still spectacular, with the massive Ben Klibreck range rising steeply from the north west side of the lochs. Directly below where I stood, the water of the small Loch Gaineamhach, trapped on the high shoulder above Loch a' Bhealaich, displayed the most magnificently deep royal blue colour, contrasting markedly with the pale blue of the sky beyond and above (Plate 15). My vantage point was a rounded, grassy and rocky, tundra-topped hill and was split by the boundary between Lairg parish to the west and Farr parish to the east. I walked off the top, following a former fence line down its south-eastern flank, marked by its old rusty iron posts, the wires from which became detached long ago and now lay twisted and rusted on the ground.

As spectacular as the views had been from the small summit, it was a bit of a relief to get away from the unrelenting, strong biting wind at that exposed height. The old fence line led to a dry peat-hagged bealach, which drained north from here into Loch a' Bhealaich and south into the drainage basin of Strath Tirry. As I was admiring the wind and rain-sculptured peat shapes, I heard a cry in the distance, in the direction of the loch, which sounded like what I can only describe as a donkey being strangled! It was a high pitched, painful-sounding whine and the only living thing I could think of it belonging to at such a remote outpost was a Golden Eagle. I scoured the far side of the loch (without my recently departed binoculars, which would have been handy at this instant!), but could see nothing to give me a clue to where, or from what, the sound was coming. I took some pictures on my digital camera and then zoomed into them on the screen, but I still could not detect the maker of the strange noise. A little frustrated in not having my inquisitiveness satisfied, I carried on, up the next, final slope of the day towards the great holy grail of the trip, the source my local river, the River Brora.

The notion of seeking out the source of the Brora, marked on the map as no more than an extensive boggy area and a small lochan, Loch Dabhaich, first came to me when I was preparing for the trip at home. I wanted to visit it for no other reason than just curiosity, which, in reality, is exactly why I undertook the whole expedition in the first place! So, when I was walking up the grassy slope, which had been rilled with small burns dissecting the deep peat and draining directly downslope into the Allt Meall na Teange, I began to get mildly excited at reaching another significant landmark on the journey. It wasn't just the fact that I was going to view where water collected for the uppermost reach of my local river, the same spot also marked the start of the last segment of my trip, by crossing the final main watershed. The remainder of my walk from this point to home would all be within the Brora drainage basin.

It was to be a while before I reached the top of this hillside, as I became distracted by wildlife - again! For the majority of the trek, but especially so on this day, I had seen many, many Common Lizards underfoot. All you generally see is a quick flash of movement out of the side of your eye in the heather or moss, as the small reptile is disturbed from its leisurely sunbathing by your passing. Mostly, the escape is a speedy wiggle, a quick scurry and that's all you see. Sometimes, after the first reactive dash, before they completely disappear, they stop to check that the threat is still present, by which time, if you have stopped too, you can get a rare chance to observe

Britain's, as its name implies, commonest lizard. In fact, probably if it wasn't for the protected conservation status applied to its slightly larger cousin, the Sand Lizard, it may well have become Britain's only legged lizard, the only other British lizard being the legless Slow Worm.

Anyway, I had engaged in this stand-off routine with several lizards over the walk, but never had been able to get a picture of a single one. On every previous occasion, as soon as I got my camera into position and ready to shoot, each lizard frustratingly turned tail and quickly disappeared. Lizards abounded on this particular west-facing hillside and I decided to have another go. Those on this slope (it was 5.15 and still the sun was strong) appeared to be less camera-shy and remained in place for a while longer, allowing me the time to prepare my camera and I managed to spend a few minutes photographing two willing subjects. Being cold-blooded, they bask in the sun until their blood temperature reaches 30°C, before they begin to hunt on their prey of mainly insects. Usually they are around 10-16cm in length and my first subject fell into the low end of this category, but my second was a whopper, and *he* posed for me until *I* had had enough!

He was about 16cm long and, although he was scaly all over, his head was smooth, and his back was a bit more textured. His scaly tail was so comparatively rough, it was like a whole series of small badminton shuttlecocks all stacked together in the same direction. His torso was a pale khaki colour, with a wide, brown side-stripe running from his upper jaw, through his eyes and down along his flanks and his quite distinct scaly tail was more of a pale green colour. His camouflage was absolutely superb for this terrain; looking through the camera at the outset, I frequently could not actually even see him, and only took a picture knowing he was in the frame somewhere. He allowed me to get very close and I don't really know why; he was just a bold creature and I was grateful that he was, as the pictures of him I took are better than I could ever have usually hoped for. I was able, not only to get shots looking down on him from above, but he let me move around so I could take some others looking at him directly in the face. Some courageous lizard, he was, or maybe a bit dim; he would have made a fine snack for a fox!

Once again, I set off pleased with my sightings and photographic achievements; by now you'll have realised it doesn't take too much to keep me happy! I rejoined the line of the old fence and more deer, part way up the dissected hillside, retreated in their usual panicky fashion, as I advanced up the slope. Deer really do move in a funny way. They don't just gallop off, like horses do when they race, they 'pronce' in a fashion more like horses in a dressage ring; their heads and ears are held back and their thin fore-legs come very high off the ground. It always amuses me, as it looks so uncool! Alone again, close to the top and I gazed back to the west, towards the ground I'd walked across over the previous few days. It was a hazy view at this time in the evening sunshine and it was about to be my final view of Ben Hee, as the slope finally shallowed out close to the final summit of my day.

By 6.00, I had reached the flat top and marched towards a small, natural mound on the plateau, around 2m above the rest of the terrain, across which the old fence line ran. On top of the mound, standing next to an old gnarled, wind-sculptured, wooden fence-post, I was greeted with my final new vista of the day. It was quite a staggering scene and the colours were absolutely stunning; the beigey-greens of the moorland, the browns and greys of the hills and the rich blues of the sky. However, what really stood out most of all were the tall, stark, bright-white pylons of the new distant windfarm at Kilbraur, which was only 10km from Brora. It was still 25km away from where I was standing, but it was so clear, as the pylons simply contrasted greatly to anything else in the whole panoramic view. I was amazed at just how clear and obtrusive they were. However, very few people, if any at all, I suppose, ever get this particular view and I felt a sense of happiness and privilege that I was here witnessing this fine 360⁰ view all alone.

All alone, that is, until I was nearly forced off my perch! As if to mark my homecoming, the RAF decided to use me as an impromptu strafing target; a jet fighter screamed up from behind me, passed directly and so close above me that I could almost touch it, and raced off into the blue yonder in the east (Plate 16). Living in the north of Scotland, I am pretty much used to jets buzzing around quite frequently, but this was *something* else; I'd had almost a week of complete solitude and peace and now I was being scared to death by a pilot with an impersonal grievance against me and using me as target practice! To be slightly less melodramatic, I did actually hear it coming and tried to take a picture of it as it roared overhead, but it was over me and gone before I could get set up, so only caught it on film (well, memory card!) as it fled away to its next attack on an unsuspecting hill-walker!

With a heart-beat slowly returning to normal, I took some pictures from this high spot, which at 502m (1645ft), was actually to be my highest point on the entire trip. Around 200m in front of me, I could see Loch Dabhaich, a mostly dried-up, dark, peaty, boggy patch, which was the whole object of my being at this particular spot - and mightily unimpressive it looked too! On leaving my little pinnacle, I had immediately crossed over from the parish of Lairg into Rogart parish, in which I would be for the next 24 hours or so. I strolled over to the bog and it became strikingly colourful closer up, with its jet black, peaty mud supporting a lush perimeter growth of deep green grass and the blue sky reflecting in what little water remained in the loch.

Close up, it was a strange sight. Loch Dabhaich sat in an extensive shallow bowl, surrounded by moorland on all sides and it would have been around 100m across when full. Now, however, the water in the loch was so low, only a couple of centimetres deep in fact, that it was below the level of its outfall into the burn which, when flowing, would eventually emerge into the Moray Firth at Brora, 35km away. There were several stones and boulders poking out of the black, peaty loch bottom, as though they had been thrown into it, which they could well have been, but they could also have fallen there after being eroded from the overlying peat which had formed around them after the last Ice Age. There were a few hummocks of grass still surviving in the loch, completely isolated from the shore and, most intriguing of all, there were many deer tracks in the gloupy peat of the loch's bottom, leading from its edge towards the centre. At the end of the tracks in the peat were hollows where the deer had rolled about and wallowed, plastering themselves in peat as their anti-pest coating.

The outflow, as described earlier, at the loch's east side was dry. It was an inauspicious start for the great river of my home parish, which rose in this parish of Rogart. As it flowed from here, it wasn't *officially* the River Brora – that name only took effect at the meeting of two burns at Dalnessie, some 8km downstream from this source. In fact, this burn wasn't even named on the OS map. Immediately downstream from the loch, its channel at its beginning was quite twisty and was deeply incised into the thick peat. For a great part of its embryonic journey, it disappeared from view into dark, deep sink holes, re-emerging, in some cases, tens of metres downstream. Its route was always clearly visible on the ground surface, as there was still a small valley where it had previously flowed, over its now sub-terranean course. Above its underground passage were land bridges of various lengths and you could see where these had collapsed in places, leaving the burn exposed in a deeply cut channel. The deepest sink hole was a good 4m below the surface and the gaping cavern into which the burn entered was around 1m high and wide.

As I quickly covered the downhill ground beside the small burn, I was following in the footsteps of the early Ordnance Surveyors. They had marched down this same burn marking spot heights in

1873, in preparation for the publication of the 1:10,000 scale map in 1879. Having begun my working life at the tender age of 17 similarly as an OS surveyor, I was filled with admiration, imagining my earlier counterparts battling, in the clothing of their day, against the elements and probably the midges too. My admiration increased, as I imagined that they must have carried with them all of their bulky equipment for months on end, out in this particular rugged terrain and also the remainder of the inhospitable and inaccessible areas in the Highlands of Scotland. I don't know how they actually managed it physically, mentally and logistically, but it was such a tremendous collective achievement and something we all take so much for granted in these days of digitised mapping, GPS, aerial photography and, of course, Google Earth! They did it the hard way; the only way they had available to them - and their work still stands the test of time and, more importantly, accuracy, today. End of grovelling tribute to OS forebears!

The un-named burn gradually began to collect some water and a flow was soon apparent. As I lost height, the hills in the distance all around me disappeared below the horizon and my entire world soon became enclosed by this lonely and beautiful valley. At the joining of the first tributary, I took a refreshing drink from the water of the burn I'd been walking down and it tasted so sweet. It was on a par with, or even better than the crystal clear water of the quartzite-based burn in Srath Dionard on Day 3, but maybe I was biased now because I was on my home turf!

Continuing down the course of the burn, I became the scourge of many small groups of deer, up until then happily grazing on the good grass on the valley floor. The river was so incised into the peat, that I could walk along the river bank below the main surface level of the valley floor and get near enough to the unsuspecting beasts to get some good close up photos. Bog fir stumps had been commonly exposed in the peat sides of the river banks (Plate 17), the banks being in some cases around 4m high. In places, the river had cut down through the thick peat drape to expose the underlying glacial boulder clay, on which the organic matter originally colonised after the Ice Age and from which the peat formed.

The colours again in the evening sunshine were so fresh and starkly contrasting along the river banks. The deep blue reflection of the paler blue skies on the surface of the water; the lush green strips of grass on the narrow river terraces; the dark red-brown, dry peat bank sides, all encompassed by the khaki-browns of the surrounding valley sides would have been a landscape painter's dream!

I was expecting to stumble across a fair bit of archaeology along the sides of the burn, but I only found a single possible shieling site. It was not conclusive by any means, as it was a rough rectangle of 0.4m high linear grassy mounds, measuring 4.5m x 3m, and it appeared to have one end open towards the river. It was set in a nice spot, on a raised dry patch on the east bank of the river, and there was plenty of narrow grazing available all along the valley downstream of here.

I came across a fine, discarded 5-pointed Red Deer antler, about 45cm (18") long, on the river bank just after I got going again and decided to take it as a wee souvenir of my trip. By this time, it was 7.40 and my mind turned to thinking of where to camp. I was making for a meeting of three un-named burns at a point describing this exactly in Gaelic – Bun nan Tri-allt (The Foot of Three Rivers). The combined waters then became the Allt Gobhlach (The Forked or Pronged River) as it flowed south towards the lodge at Dalnessie. Around 1.5km downstream of the triple point, I found a suitable campsite and relieved my shoulders of their burden. It was a wide, flat grassy river terrace at a broad, bend in the river curving through 90^0 and, while in a fairly exposed setting, it just seemed perfect, especially as the wind had dropped completely in this part of the valley. I quickly had my tent up and was tucking into my meal before I knew it, while listening to the commentary of Glasgow Rangers' defeat in the UEFA

Cup Final in Manchester on my small transistor radio, the reception from which was almost as good as home.

I had walked only around 15km in total today, but had trudged over 5 passes or shoulders, so it had been quite gruelling in parts. I'd had some magnificent sights and thrills (the jet fighter comes to mind as a thrill!) and had supped from the source of the River Brora. I had caught a glimpse of almost home and was now camped in a lovely spot beside a slow-flowing part of the Allt Gobhlach, where the wind had ceased for the first time on the entire trip, so it was very, very peaceful. I sat out on the side of the river bank eating my pasta, watching the occasional small fish rise, in the still of the evening, delightfully without the presence of even a single midge. I was around 7km from the nearest road and 8km from the nearest habited dwelling. All was perfect in my own, isolated little world.

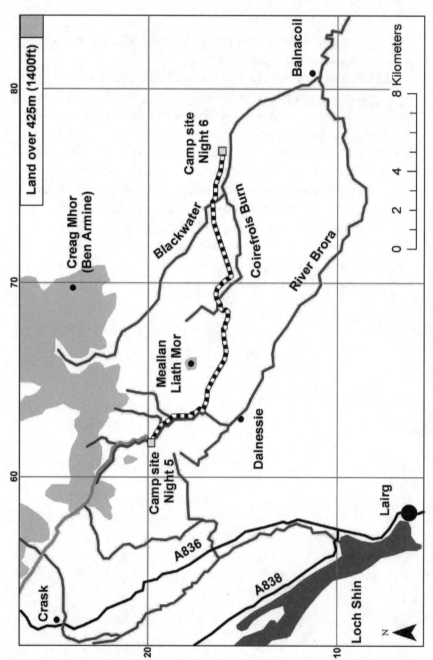

Day 6 Route - Allt Gobhlach to Gobernuisgach

8

DAY 6: ALLT GOBHLACH TO GOBERNUISGACH

The penultimate day of my trip dawned and I was up sharp at 7.40. It was a grey morning; definitely cooler and with less wind than on previous mornings and there had been an overnight dew. I could just see on the skyline that the top of Ben Klibreck was in cloud. My exposed campsite had served me well and I was packed and ready by 8.50, ready for a slog; my morning times were getting better! I had to cover quite a lot of ground today to get to the River Skinsdale, in my home parish of Clyne, where I was aiming to camp that night.

Unsurprisingly, by 9.30, I had come to a stop! Over the previous few days, I had seen many examples of Lousewort and now I had been confronted with a bit of an anomaly. Not 50cms from an example of the usual pink-flowered variety stood, undoubtedly, another Lousewort, yet this one's flower petals were as white as white could be. It was exactly the same shape and size, but the colouring was so different. I had to double take, then noted where it was and took some photographs. A few metres further on there was another, then another and finally another, this latter one appeared to be actually growing from the same root as its pink cousin a centimetre away (Plate 18). Its leaves were bright green, contrasting to the leaves of the pink-flowered 'commoner', which had a strong tinge of purple to it, exactly like the leaves of a Lollo Rosso lettuce. I have since discovered that white varieties of Lousewort are very rare indeed and I felt very happy to have discovered this particular colony, the details of which have now been safely lodged with Scottish Natural Heritage.

Feeling on a high once more at being at the (small, Nick Lindsay-scale) frontier of discovery, I pressed on down the banks of the Allt Gobhlach, which had exposed bare, heavily weathered and now friable granite rock, directly beneath the overlying peat, in its river bed. Soon, I was at the end of the Allt Gobhlach, at its confluence with the An Crom-allt, which flowed from the north east. In the cleft between the two burns stood a small, wooden sheep-shearing bothy, measuring only 4m x 3.3m. It didn't appear on the OS 2nd edition map of 1906 and I don't think it is used nowadays, as part of its corrugated iron roof had been blown off and its door, facing to the south, was wide open to the elements. I had to take my high rucksack off to get through the door, as the entrance was quite low. Inside, it was subdivided into two by a planking wall and there were two benches in one part. There was also much 'organic' evidence that sheep had used the bothy as a shelter in recent years, and many people had also visited it over time, as witnessed by their name-carvings and written graffiti on the wooden interior walls.

If the dates of the graffiti are to be believed, and I don't see why they shouldn't be, some of them go back to the 1920s. The earliest I could find was carved quite carefully in seriffed capitals into a horizontal cross-member; TOMMY MURRAY MCCCCXXVI (Roman numerals for 1926), whose surname had been altered by someone over the years to MOBBAY. This name was next to DOLLY ADAM, BRORA and maybe the pair had spent some time here; who knows? In a similar, old fashioned lettering style were the names ROBERT ROSS, GOLSPIE and CHARLES M^{C}LEOD, GOLSPIE. Amongst the other names on the walls were two in pencil from the Red Deer Commission in Inverness - I Mackay and D Sutherland in February 1966 – and I thought to myself that it would have been a very cold time of year to have been roaming in these remote parts carrying out surveys on the deer. There was an ANGUS MACKENZIE, ROGART, 9th August 1949, a Donald Renwick, from what strangely looked like 'China', in 1938, a WILLIE ROSS and ALISTAIR GORDON, 17.9.53 and a William Ross from Big Barns, Dunrobin, Golspie in July 1956. These were the main names with old dates attached to them, although there were other, more recent ones left by walkers, such as Helger Braatz from West Germany in 1981 and (I might be wrong, but) probable poachers (RF, WB and 'ATTY AND IAN'), who had boasted that 'STAGS ARE WHERE YOU FIND THEM. WE ALWAYS FIND SOME', followed by a series of years they must have visited here from 1989 to 1999.

I crossed over the An Crom-allt and walked for a while along a track which had been made boggy by estate all-terrain vehicles in wetter weather. On a flat stretch by the widening river plain, I came across a 'deer lick', which is basically a large cube of solid mineral concentrate, set on a stick in the ground for the deer to lick at during the long winter months, kindly provided by the estate. Close by, clambering slowly over a luxuriant green patch of sphagnum moss, I came across an enormous black, shiny Violet Ground Beetle (Plate 19), many of which I'd seen before, but this one didn't seem keen on getting away from me and allowed me to capture its beautiful image on my camera.

At 10.30, I came across the most substantial stone-built ruin of the whole trip so far. Standing high above the river terrace on its east bank, just off the modern day riverside track, the 19m long, 5m wide roofless building occupied a bleak, exposed site. It was marked on the 1879 map as roofed, but had become unroofed by the time of the updated edition 27 years later. It was probably built for a shepherd on Marshall and Atkinson's Great Sheep Farm of Lairg, the largest sheep farm in Sutherland, which was created in 1809 and involved the removal of hundreds of tenants whose families had occupied the area for generations. The building appeared to be of a planned, well-constructed, post-clearance style, and was divided into 3 separate segments, with doors to these all facing to the south. The skilfully and beautifully built double-skinned walls of large, originally rounded granite blocks which had been custom-shaped for the building, were 0.6m thick and stood up to 1.5m high at the rear, and there was a possible fireplace in the central compartment. It would have been a lonely life up here looking after the sheep, but I think that the house would have been quite wind and watertight and it would have been a fantastic place to raise children.

I investigated a nearby patch of grass, around 60m to the south of this building. Needless to say, this area had been habited long before the adjacent stone building, as the outline of a compact little D-shaped shieling had survived here. It measured 4m x 2.5m and its low walls of moss and heather-covered stone were spread to 0.8m wide. There was also an area of peat cuttings close by, which would have certainly been used by the inhabitants of the stone building, but may well have been started by the shieling dwellers.

Leaving this site at 11.00, I carried on down the east bank of the An Crom-allt and was soon watching one of the dozens of Common Sandpipers I'd disturbed on the trip. Always resident near water, on previous approaches, they would fly off down a river or across a loch emitting an alarming high-pitched 'Pheep-pheep-pheep-pheep', as they retreated in sheer panic. They were, therefore, never difficult to spot, but they were very difficult to photograph. Strangely, this particular bold specimen flew off, but landed on a boulder in the middle of the river soon after. I had just taken what was still a fairly long-distance picture of it, from around 25-30m away, when I caught sight of a splash out of the corner of my eye just downstream. My gaze was completely taken by an image of a dark object moving effortlessly upstream and I forgot all about the posing Sandpiper, which may well have evacuated the spot with its 'pheep-pheep-pheep' for all I was now aware!

This is where you, the reader, first came in at the start of this mono-logue; it was the Otter hunting for fish. I was absolutely transfixed! I'd seen otters occasionally before, but these sightings had always been on the coast. One time, around 1986, I spotted one in the kelp just off the shoreline at Onich, south of Fort William, feasting casually on its back in the water on a freshly caught salmon. I watched it, just as transfixed then as now, from behind a rock on the shore, as it com-pletely devoured its prey, but I can't now remember whether I had my camera available at that time. This time, my camera was already out and operational and I used my stick as a mono-pod to avoid cam-era-shake, to try and compensate for all my excitement. I just took as many shots as I could, but a ripple moving upstream from 25m just wouldn't win many photographic awards! It continued to glide grace-fully upstream, with its small head peering out of the water now and again, until it reached a large boulder on the bank on the far side of the river.

To my sheer amazement, it clambered out of the river onto the boulder and stood on all fours in a crouched position staring directly at me, with its bushy whiskers looking like a Mexican moustache. It couldn't have been too bothered by this alien in its world returning its stare, as it soon splashed back into the 5 or 6m wide river and continued foraging upstream. When it did come into contact with its prey, there would be an almighty thrash and splash as it chased it for a moment, then it would just continue on in a smooth fashion once again. It must have been at least over a metre long (4ft) from nose to tail, and its hind quarters and tail looked so powerfully built. It may well have been a male. I felt mighty privileged again, to be witnessing this display right in front of my nose and without it apparently caring about my presence. It semi-swam and semi-crawled up a small race of rapids on the right-angled sweep in the river and I thought that it might be the last glimpse, as it submerged again, back into deeper water upstream.

How wrong could I be? At the closest spot in the river to me, it again hauled its sleek, shiny wet body and long, long tail out of the water, this time directly onto the far grassy bank opposite me and my overworking camera. It wandered about a bit, sniffed, then lifted its tail against a small boulder on the bank, scent-marked it and slunk back into the water (Plate 20), before soon disappearing a little further upstream behind a boulder and, presumably, on into its holt. 'How good was that?' I thought to myself! I waited around for probably 10 minutes, partly still pinching myself to make sure the whole show I'd witnessed had been real and partly hoping that the otter would come out again for an encore for its rapturous audience of one! I'd already had fully 5 minutes of prime-time entertainment which you just couldn't buy, but it never did re-appear to me, so, given that I had to make progress today, I had to press on. I left this theatre at 11.20, mesmerised by the whole enthralling experience. Forgivably, in this instance, I could hardly wait to phone home and contact the outside world to relate my tale!

I was still on a high when I reached the first real barrier to my progress. Less than a kilometre downstream from my 'Tarka' encounter, I was confronted with the slightly depressing sight of a high, deer fence, which had been erected around a forestry plantation. I had planned to visit the cleared township of Dail na Ceardaich, which was within the plantation, however, I abandoned this idea to avoid the difficult walking through the unchecked vegetation and young trees. Instead, I decided to skirt around the north side of the fence and aim for a pass between two small hills in the distance. This would lead down into the Coirefrois valley on the other side, where my intention was to follow the burn into my home parish of Clyne.

As I stood against the impenetrable rylock deer fence and looked towards the distant stone remains of the houses of Dail na Ceardaich, still visible above the young trees, I almost felt like it was me who'd been cleared from my home and banished from the township. It made *me* feel excluded, but I just couldn't begin to imagine what the feelings of the cleared inhabitants must have been 200 years ago, as they were made to leave their homes, sometimes forcibly. They all then faced a horribly uncertain life, either on sub-subsistence level 'lots' allocated to them on the coast, or as pioneering emigrants, and all the risks and perils which that entailed, abroad. I realised that I probably wasn't alone in this feeling of exclusion even today; there was a well-trodden path along the length of the outside of the fence line, where deer had trampled, longing for a way in to get at the lush green grass on the other side of the fence. Never was the old adage truer. In their free, roaming world, the kings of the hill used to know no barriers, as would also have been the case for the township folk, and it must be puzzling and frustrating for them to now come across a rigid obstacle, through which they are unable to pass.

I left the austere deer fence and headed for a circular, stone sheep-fold I could see at the base of the hill slope. This was set just above the open moorland and I scared another grouse, which took off in the same state of absolute panic as the others before, in the process. Strangely, the sheepfold is not marked on either the 1st or 2nd edition OS maps, but it certainly looks old enough to have been included. Anyway, I recorded it for the HER; it was 11m in diameter internally and its 1m wide stone walls stood only around 0.7m high. The walls appeared incomplete (normally they would stand around 1.5m high), but, oddly, there was not enough tumble in the vicinity to account for what was apparently missing.

As I marched up the aptly named Leathad Cas (Steep Brae) to the bealach between Meallan Liath Beag (Little Grey Hill) and Leathad na Seamraig (Slope of the Shamrock), I think I gave the same grouse, which had fled in a panic earlier for what it thought was safety, another heart-stopping scare. It's as though they really think that their world is coming to an abrupt end (on reflection, I suppose this train of thought is thoroughly justified in many cases!), as they shriek in terror and flap away in a low trajectory to escape their disturber. They certainly give any unwary visitor to their territory a bit of a heart-stopping scare too, which, in a way, I suppose, is justice!

The weather had been steadily improving during the morning and the sun was beginning to appear from behind the clouds, as I came across my first sighting on the trip of Common Butterwort. It was not yet in flower, but the pale green, starfish-shaped leaf pattern, flush with the ground gives it away every time. In flower, it has a single stem rising up to around 10cms above its base, and is tipped with a delicate lone head of purple petals pointing back down to the ground. The butterwort is one of the floral world's carnivores, trapping unwary insects on its sticky-coated leaves and these particular specimens had a selection of doomed victims encased in its larder-like leaves.

The appearance of the butterwort made me think that I hadn't seen its carnivorous partner-in-crime, Sundew, on the trip. Typically, not 20 minutes later, I came across one, just before I stopped for lunch on the top of the hill, overlooking Leathad na Seamraig. The commonly found Sundew abounds in similarly damp, boggy, nutrient-deficient habitats, and is instantly recognisable with its myriad of pink, thin, sticky-globuled fronds, surrounding its upturned 'palms' at the ends of outstretched arms, which emanate from its central root core. It is a small but very beautiful plant, stunningly intricate and ruthlessly effective, catching its unsuspecting insect prey by deceiving them into thinking its pretty, flower-like palms contain sweet nectar, rather than deadly, unforgiving adhesive. Similar to the familiar Venus Fly-Trap houseplant, the Sundew's fronds curl up around its trapped prey, which is devoured by the plant as a supplement to its supply of nutrients from its poor habitat.

Not fancying insects to supplement *my* lunch, I tucked into my more appetising, but standard, oatcakes and cheese from my sublime vantage point overlooking the long, straight, rift-like valley, 230m below me to the south-west, carrying the meandering River Brora proper (Plate 21). Not for the first time on this trip, I was in my own little heaven, as I sat next to a cairn on top of a fairly insignificant, un-named hill, but with a view to die for. To the east, I was reacquainted with a view of the windfarm at Kilbraur and to the west was the receding outline of the distant Ben Klibreck; the view to the north, however, was completely obscured by the foreground presence of Meallan Liath Beag and Meallan Liath Mor.

At this spectacular location, I just *had* to report not only the magnificence of what I was seeing at that time, but also, of course, what I'd seen earlier in the day. I took my mobile phone out to see if a signal was available. I was in luck; full coverage. Sitting beside the cairn, I can see myself now, euphorically relating my position and experiences to Jacquie at 'Mission Control' and also my father. After the calls had finished, the realisation that it would only be the following evening when I would be back at home, properly kicked in. My adventure was nearing its end and my previous elation transformed itself into a slight sadness.

Getting a grip of myself, I was just about to set off when I noticed a 'pellet' on the far side of the cairn. Pellets are the regurgitated, indigestible material, such as bones and fur, left by birds of prey, as well as other carrion-scavenging birds. This particular one was quite large, measuring about 8cm long and 3cm in diameter and had probably been disgorged by an owl. The dried out pellet contained several small bones, bits of feather quill, beak and claw and a very strange orange coloured, breast-plate-shaped item. It was extra-specially interesting (if you can get turned on by a glorified fur-ball!) in that it also contained some grains of quartz, slightly smaller than pea-sized, derived from the weathered granite bedrock strewn about this hill-top. These must either have been accidentally consumed with its prey, whilst the bird's mind was firmly focussed on guzzling its meal, or deliberately ingested as an aid to digestion. Maybe it was a bit of both.

So, with the pellet safely packed in a plastic bag for further, amateur forensic examination at home (I obviously *can* get turned on by said glorified fur-ball!), I strode down the south east side of the bealach. I was heading towards my next target of Loch an t-Slugaite (Loch of the Miry Pool?) and I passed by an old 'Gelert' thermal glove, accidentally dropped possibly by a stalker on a hunting expedition or a fisherman walking to a remote, isolated hill-top loch; who knows? If you are the owner of the mislaid glove, I can tell you exactly where to find it!

On the lower ground, still some way off the loch, I had walked over an area of Dwarf Birch, growing flat with the ground, with its fresh, bright green, delicately-lobed leaves stretching skywards. In this low, almost crouched, attitude, it could just about survive in what would often be harsh conditions in these hills. As I made my way closer towards the loch, I could see that it was teeming with fish (possibly the glove belonged to a fisherman, after all), which were constantly breaking the surface, leaving their tell-tale rings ever spreading concentrically outwards from their origin. There were also three pairs of Widgeon (a species of duck), gliding about on the loch, which was quite low and reedy at its edges. The males make a strange call, a sort of 'Whee-eeze, whee-eeze' and sounded (for those of a certain age and for the want of a better description) just like Mr McEnery on his bike in the Magic Roundabout!

Approaching the banks of the loch, I could see the reason why the fish were having a feeding frenzy; clouds of flies were dancing in the warm sunshine around the loch and many were providing the fish with a reward for their out-of-water activities. Unperturbed by the fish, the widgeon moved to the safety of the centre and the far side of the loch, as they certainly *were* perturbed by this stranger on the shore.

Loch an t-Slugaite was fed at its upstream end by the Coirefrois Burn and the same burn continued downstream out of the loch too. I refreshed my water bottle in the rocky outfall of the loch and tramped down the south bank. The burn had an unusual morphology, being very wide and slow-flowing in places, for such a relatively small burn. At parts where the gradient increased, the expanse was filled with boulders, which would have formed rapids in full spate. The burn flowed into sections which were really small lochans and these, too, were teeming with fish. I snapped away with my camera, trying to get an 'arty' photograph of the rings on the still water's surface. However, it wasn't until I was back home viewing my digital images that I realised I'd actually captured a fish leaping clean out of the water, which I hadn't noticed at the time when I was there!

There were many places along the sides of the burn where the peat was falling away from the banks and getting gradually consumed by the flowing water. Frequently, at these locations, the deer had used the exposed peat sides as vertical wallowing holes to re-plaster themselves with their ritual coating of peat. The large amounts of moulted hair which had stuck to the plasticine-textured bank sides, along with their giveaway hoof-prints, of course, were testimony to this pattern of behaviour. Along these peat bank sides, there were many more bog fir stumps exposed and the long, horizontal roots coming from the stump centres made ideal scratching posts for the deer and also places to rub their antlers, as witnesses by the grooves and gouges on the exposed old timber. One exceptionally long horizontal root branch extended amazingly for over 4m, hanging unsupported out of the side of the bank.

As time, and I, marched on, I discovered the old footings of a former dwelling, in a rough, grassy angle between an adjoining tributary and the main Coirefrois Burn. The stone remains stood around 0.6m high, but the sturdier gable ends in many ruins often stand higher and this was no exception. The ruin was built against the furthest set back river terrace bank and the outline of a smaller, less substantial building lay on the terrace above. Neither of these buildings, strangely, was marked on either of the early OS map editions, even though the surveyors had definitely passed this way taking spot-heights along the valley floor.

The walls of the main building comprised a single skin and single course of large, rounded, unworked granite boulders and the whole building measured 10.5m x 4m. The main section had two internally connecting compartments, but a compartment at the far end was only accessible from outside. The compartment was strange, as its outer wall face was rectangular but its inner face, formed from the largest granite boulders, was circular. It looked like an original feature, so it could have been some form of crude corn-drying kiln or, less likely, it possibly was a later adaptation to form a small lambing pen. Unfortunately, over the centuries, some of the walling had tumbled and some of the key relationships needed to determine what was actually going on had been obscured. Incidentally, growing on the granite boulders was a rich and diverse range of lichen, which had enjoyed an uninterrupted growth of probably at least 2 centuries, including the spectacular red-headed, matchstick-like *Cladonia polydactyla* and the frilly grey *Parmeliopsis ambigua*.

In the days of a few centuries ago, way up in the remote hills, it was possible for the local inhabitants to often escape the laws of the land. One of the most profitable pastimes, which gave one of the most enjoyable rewards, was the illicit distilling of highly prized whisky. Occasionally, the sites of the stills, which would have been in extremely well-camouflaged bothies along the banks of small burns, can be found even today, although, by their very nature they do not easily reveal themselves. Those, of course, which were discovered by the Excise men were instantly destroyed, however, you can just imagine that corruption was rife in those days and it is possible that many a blind eye was turned, for a substantial bribe of the life-giving '*Uisge Beatha*'.

I stumbled across one such possible illicit whisky still, just 150m downstream of the stone building, at the joining of the tributary. It was almost circular and made use of existing large boulders which were already there in situ, supplemented by smaller ones added to make a continuous internal wall, and it only measured 2.1m x 1.8m. The walls were made to form a stone-lined bowl, set below the ground surface but now open to the elements. In the growing season it was clear that this area was completely overgrown by bracken and, when in functioning use, the bothy would have been covered by a camouflaged thatch, and a retractable pipe would have extended to the burn for the still's water supply.

A little further downstream, I came across a sight that made me happy that I wasn't walking upstream! A fully grown adult stag lay dead and decomposing, in the middle of the 5m wide burn. The bedraggled corpse lay mostly out of the water, grounded on rocks due to the low level of the burn, and its upper side had been a bonanza of a feast for carnivores. Beneath its exposed rib cage it was hollow, except for the herbivorous contents of its stomach, which were like the contents of a huge lawn mower bucket. The poor creature probably came to grief a few weeks ago; maybe it broke its ankle or leg crossing the burn and struggled for life, or maybe it even died of natural causes where it fell. Either way it was well dead, and must have been giving the water downstream something of an unusually meaty taint!

Continuing on down the contaminated burn, I soon came across another ridiculously-sited dandelion plant. Its bright yellow flower first attracted my attention, as it sprouted from in between two enormous boulders in the middle of the burn. Again, I was baffled as to how it could have reached such a remote location, and it shared its crevice with some small bilberry plants too. It never ceased to amaze me how hardy and resilient some species of plant are, and the dandelion certainly slots into this category.

My progress downstream was again halted by another deer fence running across the burn, attached to which was a blue plastic fence suspended above the water, again to prevent the ingress of deer or livestock down the burn channel. It marked the boundary to a forestry plantation around another old township, Coirefrois, which I had also planned to visit. I knew that the fence was likely to be there, as I'd been consulted for information several years ago by Cathy Dagg, the archaeological contractor engaged to carry out the site's pre-afforestation survey. There was a gate, through which I could have entered, but I chose to amend my plans and abandon the visit to the township, due to the awkward walking posed by the unchecked vegetation and deep pock-marks made for the trees. The HER (Ref: MHG11141) records very little detail about the township but, being privy to some inside information, I can reveal that there are five building outlines and several enclosures within the township! The plantation was so extensive that it had also subsumed two other neighbouring pre-clearance townships, 2km and 4km respectively to the east.

As with the previously encountered ring-fenced township of Dail na Ceardaich, 7km to the west, I decided to walk where the deer had again trampled a well-worn path, while they enviously looked in to the inaccessible feast on the other side. It was now past 6.00, and I had a long trudge ahead of me over the seemingly endless, broad, moorland ridge of Blar nan Coileach (Moor of the Cock). The wind was getting to be quite cold on this exposed part and even the sun had disappeared, although it appeared to be shining in the distance all around. I tramped for around 3km along a 10m wide 'corridor' between the modern deer fence on my right and an old parallel fence-line, of both iron and wooden posts, on my left.

At some indeterminate point towards the east end of this ridge on this indistinct bog, I crossed, ingloriously, into the parish of Clyne. I could now see the familiar outlines of my local hills across the plantation's young trees in the foreground: the perfectly pyramidal peak of Ben Smeorail, with its contrastingly shaped, giant broad-backed, neighbour, Col Bheinn, dwarfing it in the background. It's strange what goes through your mind when you're on your own, on a journey like this. I was home, or almost home, and felt a twinge of sadness as I entered territory which was not new to me, and the consequent opportunity of discovery was a diminishing prospect.

However, something new I *did* find, while I was trudging the ridge. The ground was interspersed with peat hags and small peaty channels. The walking was irregular and the going was not smooth. In some of the channels and small pools on the top, the water had largely evaporated during the recent dry spell and, in many of these dried up hollows, there were examples of bright green, circular, slightly lumpy 'pancakes' on the now dry surface. It was clear that this is what happens to frogspawn when it is laid in this type of fragile environment; in unusually arid conditions, it just dries up, along with the water in which it was laid. Thousands upon thousands, probably millions, even, of tiny black gelatinous dots had all succumbed to the same fate of complete, irreversible dehydration. It seemed such a waste.

At last I was down onto the new, well-made, gravelled estate track at Dalbreck, linking the remote shooting lodge of Ben Armine, to the north west, with the public road at Sciberscross, to the south. I luckily found a place where I managed to hop from boulder to boulder across the not inconsiderable Black Water River, as I was aiming for a camping spot at any suitable spot between here and Gobernuisgach, on the River Skinsdale, around 3km further on. As it was now nearly 8.00 and my feet were definitely feeling blistered, I was longing to stop.

On the north side of the Black Water, the southern extent of the mature forestry plantation on Pollie Hill was close to the river, so my route was determined for me in walking along the outside of the forest fence, across undulating terrain covered in grass, some of which was quite long. The fence did nothing to keep deer out, as it had long since collapsed in many places along its length and been breached by them for comfortable shelter. Part way along, I could see smoke rising from the ground outside the normally uninhabited shepherd's cottage at Amat, downstream on the opposite side of the river. This was disappointing; the shepherd must have been staying there during the lambing and it meant that, as I didn't really want to camp within sight of 'civilisation', I would have to continue on beyond, out of sight of the cottage to the end of the plantation, still a good couple of kilometres away.

Having walked through patches of long grass and reeds, I checked my trouser legs for ticks and found to my dismay, that they were covered in them. There were a variety of sizes, from single large adults, up to 5mm across, to myriads of tiny larvae, less than the size of a pinhead. I do not like ticks. In fact, I despise them. It is a mystery to me why they are on this planet at all! I can find in the literature only scant references to predators of the tick, these being some species of birds, ants and beetles. Bring these predators on, I say!

Ticks can survive without feeding for months on end, but once they latch on to their unsuspecting victim, usually a deer or a sheep in this terrain, but me in this particularly rewarding case, they can gorge on the host's blood for days. The method of how ticks latch on to their hosts is known as 'questing'; that is, they wait patiently, for as long as it takes, at the tops of stalks of grass, reeds or bracken, clinging on with their rear legs, front legs extended outwards into space. When a potential hot-blooded meal comes along, their hooked fore-legs latch on, then they crawl upwards, always upwards, until they find a suitable, usually hidden, moist spot, such as under arms or the groin. There they begin to feed by inserting their voracious hypostome, a blood-sucking tube, into the skin, undetected by its victim, by using an injection of local anaesthetic and an anti-coagulant to keep the blood flowing. They can stay there attached and feeding for several days, just gorging themselves before they simply drop off and digest, at leisure, their meal in their enormously bloated bodies, swollen by their feeding frenzy. Given their technique, mode of operation and pure resilience, I grudgingly suppose that they have to be admired, but I still don't like them!

Questing on the majority of long stalks of dried grass, I did, indeed, notice ticks in their droves, patiently waiting for a host. In the past, I have had ticks crawling on me many, many times and also had them attached to me on several occasions, but I had never before seen them waiting to spring into action. Normally, you only notice them when they are crawling up your trouser legs. The risk of being infected with the nerve-affecting Lyme's Disease bacteria, of which they are unsuspecting carriers, appears to be getting greater, so it is advisable to keep a watchful eye out for them and try and prevent them getting to your skin. One of the best ways, in the first instance, is to wear light trousers, so that when they inevitably do attach themselves to your legs, they are easily spotted and brushed off. Also the simple solution of either tucking the bottoms of your trouser-legs into socks or wearing gaiters provides a good barrier between the little parasites and your skin; they do not burrow through close-weave clothing.

Seeing that my route passed unavoidably through large areas of long, tick-infested grass, I brought another anti-tick foil into play. My telescopic walking stick, which had been unbelievably useful as a walking aid, also proved its use as a grass-swishing, tick-loosening device ahead of my path. I was very pleased with this particular innovation of mine and had noticeably fewer of the little, good for nothing (as far as I could see) freeloaders, after I began putting this method into practice. I spent some time taking photographs of the wee beasties, clinging to grass stalks in their hope to hitch a ride and get a free meal. It was a very difficult proposition trying to focus the camera on a thin stalk of grass being blown in the wind, on which there were 3 or 4 black parasitic blobs in the foreground. However, I solved the problem by putting my hand directly behind the grass to give the field of view a larger focus point. It worked a treat and I now have a good picture of the wee brutes (Plate 22)!

The fading, beautifully bright, low evening sunshine shone onto the hills to the east in front of me, contrasting richly with the hills in dark shadow behind and the even darker grey skies beyond. I had reached the cleared township of Gobernuisgach and all I wanted to do was stop, take my rucksack off and rest my sore feet. The walk was beginning to take its toll on my feet, and I could feel some specific sore points on the tops of my toes and on the soles, which I presumed were blisters. I think my boots were flexing too much and this is how blisters were forming on the upper sides of my toes.

While I was passing through the township, even though it was almost 9.00, I had to take a wee look around the remains of the main building there, with strong, stone boulder walls still standing up to 2m high. It was set on a raised, undulating grassy knoll, and the building remains extended for an incredible 40m in length. It was one of the largest longhouses I had seen, and this one had something even more unique to all of my previous archaeological observations. The building had a large outshot projecting to the north, close to its west end. Nothing too unusual about that in itself, but the outshot gable end contained a fireplace, above which was a huge lintel, and I had never before seen these features in an outshot. I seemed to have spent much of this trip being pleased, and this was no exception, even though I had just been plagued by ticks and my body was aching, some parts more than others! I took some photos and then marched around the corner of the plantation to look for a place to camp, out of sight of the shepherd at Amat.

As the sun continued to sink lower in the sky, the shadows on the hills lengthened and it made for a wonderful sight at the end of the day. What also made a wonderful site was where I eventually decided to pitch my tent. I was getting to be a bit paranoid about spending my last night in such a tick-infested locality, when I spied a small, flat grassy island in the middle of the Skinsdale River. I thought not too many deer and certainly very few, if any, sheep would ever visit the island, around which the river split in two channels of some 6m width. I hopped as gingerly as I could across the only rocky crossing place to examine the area and was pleased to find the grass was short and apparently tick-free, as I'd hoped. So, my campsite for the night was to be an island refuge in the Washing Pool, a named fishing pool on the River Skinsdale, around 300m upstream of its confluence with the Black Water. My only slight concern was that if it rained heavily in the hills overnight (there was a worsening forecast), with any significant rise in the river level I could be left marooned on my own island. I thought the risk was worth taking; the alternative would have been to share the night with armies of blood-hungry ticks. No contest!

With my tent pitched for the last time on this trip, my routine was getting slicker. I quickly had my final evening meal cooked and ate it sitting on the river bank, as the sun finally disappeared from the eastern hills at 9.30. There were still no midges about, which was a blessing after the ticky end to the day. I wrote my diary when I was all snuggled in my sleeping bag and reckoned I had covered 18km today. Tomorrow, I would have to cover a similar distance to get home, with the majority of the walking being on hard tracks or roads. I wasn't really looking forward to the effect this was likely to have on my feet, but it was the last leg of the journey and I was damned if anything was going to prevent me from completing my expedition in style!

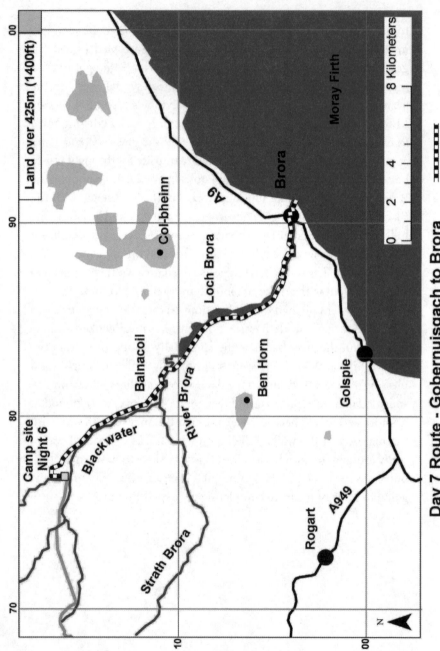

Day 7 Route - Gobernuisgach to Brora

9

DAY 7: GOBERNUISGACH TO BRORA

The final day dawned and, as I unzipped my tent to discover the state of the weather, I was delighted to find I hadn't been marooned by rivers in spate on my little island. There had been no rain overnight, but the skies were pretty grey and there was a layer of cloud obscuring the tops of the surrounding hills. Definitely, by far, the worst day, but not bad in reality and no rain so far.

I had my breakfast and packed up my tent and, while I was doing so, I caught sight of 3 cuckoos (2 blue males and one brown female) fluttering about over the plantation beside my campsite to the west. The two males, needless to say, were chasing the female and one of them was getting very racy! He was uttering a cry in flight that I'd not heard before; it was a kind of staccato version of the normal familiar cuckoo cry, sounding like 'cuck-cuck-cuck-cuck-cuck-cuckoo'. Incidentally, it is only the male who cries its famous call, which heralds the arrival of spring. This, of course, was not the first one I'd heard this year; that honour went to one close to my home in early April and I'd heard a few on this trip. After a while of displaying their aerobatic talents they disappeared over the plantation, continuing their chase and excited calling and one of these males would, I'm sure, have consummated his plan!

Because it was a gloomy morning and I'd heard on my radio that rain was forecast for the north, I debated about going up the Skinsdale to look at the cleared township of Foik, in the opposite direction to home. The old township is located on the east side of the banks of the Skinsdale, which rises 10km further to the north west, under the shadow of Ben Armine, at 704m, the highest point in my home parish of Clyne. I eventually decided I would risk the consequences of getting soaked and trudging home in the wet, and make the detour. In the end, it was just too close to not take the opportunity, so, I walked the ¾ kilometre upstream to the ruins. I was glad I did. The township contained the stone ruins of 4 buildings (the largest being 33m long), 1 corn-drying kiln, 2 enclosures, many clearance cairns, several 'tattie-pits' (holes in well-drained ground, in which potatoes were stored) and a post-clearance sheep fold. I spent till midday recording and photographing all of the features, which were still remarkably well preserved.

After completing my task in improving weather, the sun actually appeared from behind the grey clouds for a while and I set off on the long march home at 11.30. The gently-sloping sides of the Skinsdale valley make it very wide, as is its river, which is normally quite shallow, but it was even more so as a result of the recent dry spell. In fact, in many places, the water was scarcely visible and the bare bedrock and boulders of the river bed gave the impression that the course of the river was almost dry. There was a profusion of Common Vetch growing along the banks of the river and this was the first time I'd seen it on the whole trip. Still seeing new things, after all, on the final day!

On reaching the estate track from Balnacoil Lodge, which extends around 2.5km further up the valley to Muiemore, I took a long look up the valleys of the Skinsdale and the Black Water at their confluence. The valleys are quite similar, and their rivers combine to flow south east into the River Brora, just below Balnacoil. The fishing in these parts is still fair, but nowhere near, I understand, as good as it was a couple of generations ago. It's a bit like the grouse shooting; these are two blood sports which really took off in the Victorian era. The gentry of the day were suddenly able to take the opportunity to come to what had hitherto been a remote area, when the Highland Railway was extended from Ardgay to reach Helmsdale in 1871. In recent years both pastimes have declined, due, amongst other external factors, to the severe shortage of the actual end product, the grouse and the salmon. Deer numbers, however, *are* increasing, but, ironically, the popularity of deer stalking appears to be on the wane.

As I walked along the hard, stony track, I opted to walk along the centre, as there was frequently a narrow strip of grass there and this was much more comfortable for my feet. I passed the small townships of Dailamhadaidh and Dalvoran on the opposite, west side of the Black Water, as I made for the locally famous township of Achness, on the east side. It was here, in April 1821, that the last, futile resistance to the Sutherland Clearances of the early 19th Century took place: the so-called Achness Riots, culminating with the imprisonment of the ringleader, John Matheson, in Dornoch Jail for 6 months. The riot was quelled by soldiers, and there were 9 arrests, however Matheson was the only one tried. The cleared township is now silent and peaceful and the stone footing remains of 4 buildings still stand, clinging tenuously to the hillside on either side of the track.

A little south of here, below the neighbouring township of Rinscan, whose inhabitants were also involved in the riots, the Black Water undergoes a striking change in its appearance. The broad, shallow valley through which the river had previously been gently flowing, suddenly narrows and the water is channelled dramatically through a narrow neck, in a series of plunging waterfalls and on into a deep gorge. There are several vantage points for impressive views of the gorge from the track and I made good use of these on my way down towards Strath Brora.

Further down, beyond where the track departs away from the valley bottom and the river itself is no longer in sight, the spectacular, Iron Age broch of Castle Cole comes into view, sitting on a small ridge overlooking the deep Black Water gorge below. It really is an amazingly beautiful and so skilful a construction, especially considering it is around 2000 years old and still stands to around 10ft high today. It is unusually small for a broch, which are generally now regarded as being status symbols, rather than as purely defensive structures, as formerly thought. The logic behind this hypothesis is that many are just not *in* defensive positions; however, Castle Cole certainly is an exception to this, with a deep vertical drop into the Black Water on its west and a rise up from boggy moorland on all other sides. Its setting could certainly be classed as defensive!

Its stone walls are metres thick and they still survive to 3m high on its east side, but unfortunately, some of its western walling is missing, having collapsed into the deep gorge below. The broch measures only around 10m in diameter internally, smaller than some contemporary hut circles even, and its small entrance, 1.5m high and 0.7m wide, on its southern side is still perfectly preserved, and is topped by a huge boulder acting as a lintel. Internally, it has some chambers between its inner and outer skins, and several aumbries (built-in recessed shelves) are still visible on its inner face.

I took several photos of Castle Cole from the track, including some with a backdrop of the new Kilbraur windfarm, which was an interesting, if somewhat bizarre mix of the really old and the really new. Even from this distance of 5km, the stark, white towers, nacelles and blades dominated the landscape and dwarfed the broch. I wonder which of these objects will still be here in another two millennia?

As I approached Balnacoil, the full extent of the windfarm became apparent. There were 19 towering columns in the whole complex and they rise quite majestically, but quite obtrusively, from the barren moorland and hillsides. There has been much controversy over their construction, mainly in relation to their insensitive appearance in the landscape and their possible impact and damage they may have on wildlife, peat and archaeology. Whatever the issues, it no longer really matters, as they are there now, and they are there to stay – well, for 25 years anyway, which is the duration of their projected design lifespan.

I passed behind the lodge of Balnacoil and instantly received a signal on my mobile phone. I had been checking the signal since I left Foik, but this was the first one received. I phoned Jacquie to let her know my estimated time of arrival and also decided then that I would not just end the walk at my home, but would finish the journey at the mouth of the Brora River, thereby making it a 'coast to coast' walk and a complete River Brora start to finish (with the middle section by-passed) walk too.

I dropped down into Strath Brora, leaving the Black Water to flow into the River Brora a little further up the Strath, and crossed the Brora-Balnacoil-Rogart road at 2.00. This was only the third public road I had crossed in six and a half day's walking, over around 120km! I had my final lunch in the shelter of some trees, close to the banks of the River Brora, which I was about to rejoin. For my last lunch I had saved something 'special'– a tin of sardines, which I had carried as an 'emergency' meal. It was a bit ticky where I was sitting and also quite cold again in the wind, so I didn't hang around for long.

After I got going again, I disturbed a pair of geese who had been grazing on the grassland. They took flight, constantly squawking their indignance at having been disturbed, as they circled higher looking for a new spot to settle down at again. At Kilbraur, I crossed the narrow footway suspension bridge with some difficulty; my rucksack was wider than the gap between the cables dropping down to the walkway from the main suspension cables above, so I had to negotiate the crossing in a sort of ungainly, semi-sideways manner till I eventually got to the other side.

Now I was definitely getting near home. The top of Loch Brora came and went, as I marched down the improved track along its south west side, under the impressive craggy, sandstone cliffs of Carrol Rock. It is on the bare ledges of these cliffs, that the furthest inland-dwelling colony of the most graceful of sea-birds, the Fulmar, is found. Across the water, I could hear sounds of civilisation, to which I didn't take kindly, following my previous six fantastic, silent days spent in my own self-imposed, outback isolation. There were three or four cars on the Brora to Rogart road and I could hear and see an excavator undertaking some improvements on the steading at Gordonbush, on the opposite side of the loch.

I was still, however, seeing 'new' things of interest. The masses of whins beside the 'Narrows' on Loch Brora were spectacularly radiant yellow and the flora underneath the vertical cliffs of Carrol Rock were literally blooming! Part of the area has been fenced off as these native birch woods are designated by Scottish Natural Heritage (SNH) as a Special Site of Scientific Interest (SSSI). Without grazing by sheep and deer, the grass is long and the flora grows profusely and unchecked. Bluebells, Primroses, Wood Anemones and Bilberry are all represented and give a great splash of colour on the inside of the fence. Contrasting to the burst of life on one side of the track, there was another dead stag on the other side, on the shore of the loch, which had maybe been washed from upstream when the river was in spate in the early spring.

Another feature worthy of mention, even at this late stage was the prevalence of fox droppings! I had seen many during the trip, which I haven't previously mentioned, but I came across one on this last leg of the journey which entirely merits inclusion. It was jet black and must have been less than a centimetre in diameter, although you'll be relieved to discover it was not handled! What was fascinating, though, was that it was the curliest thing you could imagine! It was the same shape as a worm makes when you used to chop them in two as a child, if you know what I mean? All twisted and curly. Quite amazing!

After negotiating a maze of fences at Carrol Farm, it was back onto the long track connecting the farm with the outside world. A herd of young stags was grazing on the grass beside the loch and they weren't at all flustered by my passing. They were obviously fairly tame, being fed by the estate, which seems a bit unfair, when it comes to them being hunted. Unlike 'wild' deer, these specimens would not necessarily flee when approached by stalkers, making them easy kills for the estate or for paying punters. As I passed within, maybe, 10m of them, their growing, velvet-covered antlers looked so soft and furry. Once the velvet falls off, the antlers would soon have a different appearance, as this headgear becomes a serious weapon, used against rivals during the rutting season in the autumn. They were, however, all the best of pals as I strode past!

Passing underneath the craggy cliffs of Leadoch and Ducharry, I had my final classic view of Loch Brora and Carrol Rock (Plate 23). The track was easy walking, apart from the hardship on my feet, and I upped my pace as I realised I was behind my estimated time of arrival at the Harbour. I actually did some running, after I had passed through the farm gate onto the final section of the track, through the Doll Ford Woods. I emerged onto the Doll Ford road and met a lady walking three Pekinese dogs towards me. She told me that she had just seen a Roe Deer on the other side and, if I was lucky, I might see it too! This made me chuckle greatly to myself, given the fantastic variety, quantity and quality of sights I'd witnessed over the previous six days!

After I crossed the footbridge I did, indeed, glimpse the Roe, as it scampered off to take cover in the undergrowth, before I passed through the field on the north bank of the river where it had been grazing. The footpath along this side of the river had been newly improved by the local Footpath Users' Group, allowing an uninterrupted link from Brora to the loch. I was happy to use this path as the ground underfoot was soft and much easier on my feet. I passed some fishermen, casting gently into a slow pool from the opposite side of the river and I could just imagine them cursing me, as I was probably disturbing their potential catch.

All along the sides of the river, there was a further profusion of bluebells and primroses and the whins were groaning under its blooms of brilliant yellow. It had been a bumper spring for the quick-spreading bush and the whole atmosphere along the river bank was pleasantly perfumed with its beautiful, uncannily coconut-like scent. I took a short cut through a broad open field where the river took a large meandering detour. I could see that there were cows and calves in the field, but thought little more of it ... until I was about half-way across. This is when they began to take an interest in their visitor and all drifted over, as one, to investigate.

Maybe they thought that I was going to feed them or maybe they were just curious, as I strode across their territory. Or maybe it was because one of these 'cows', which was also getting close, now appeared a bit larger than its pals and it I noticed it had odd-shaped udders!!!! At that particular moment, I didn't think it had been such a good idea for me to be wearing a red, long-sleeved tee shirt, which I thought may be adding to this 'cow's' interest! I quickened my pace and noticed, out of the corner of my eye, the crofter on the skyline at the top of the river terrace, probably wondering what I was doing in his field of cows and a bull. I could imagine how amused he would have been by the scene unfolding beneath him! By now the cows were pretty close and were a bit frisky and inquisitive, but the bull, thankfully, never emerged from the herd and was just accompanying his harem, probably wondering what all the fuss was about. I leaped across a ditch and the herd didn't follow, probably disappointed that I hadn't brought them anything to dine on. I was just thankful that the bull hadn't been as interested as the cows and that I hadn't had to make a run for it!

I met the watching crofter on the track, at the top of the slope soon after. It was Hamish Ross, whom I knew, and he then realised who it was who'd just walked across his field. He didn't mention the incident and neither did I, though I probably didn't really save face, until my reply to his casual question of 'Where had I been?' met with a small amount of surprise!

I continued along the path, briskly running down the occasional slope to make up some time and eventually emerged onto the tarmac road where the old Brora coal mine used to be. The mine and all its associated buildings has long since completely disappeared, having closed down in 1974; however on this spot, since 1813 until its demise, Jurassic coal had been brought to the surface and it had the significance of being the most northerly coal mine in Britain. It is due to this geological fortitude that the whole of Brora's industrial heritage has been based. The village, in the past, has boasted a salt producing industry, a woollen mill, a brickworks and a distillery, to mention but a few, all of which existed here as they were able to take cheap advantage of the locally mined coal. Sadly, all these industries have now disappeared, except for the world famous Clynelish whisky distillery, which, however, no longer uses coal to fire its operations.

It was now 5.30, and I was around half an hour later than I had estimated! I could imagine what Jacquie would be thinking at the Harbour! As I strode gingerly on the hard surface of the public road alongside the river, I spotted Jacquie driving towards me with my mother in the passenger seat. It was all smiles as they pulled alongside and my mother's first words, typically, were 'Ooh. Didn't you take a razor with you???'

I wanted to complete the walk properly, so I carried on to my final destination of the harbour, around half a mile away. But, before I could get across the bridge carrying the A9 across the river, I was met by friends, Norman & Morag Gibson, who were passing in their car and congratulated me on my walk. My progress in Brora was stuttering and the cold wind was getting to me a bit. I met Lynne Gunn and her mother, Pam Gordon, coming out of the Spar shop, just across the bridge, and they were naturally curious about why I was carrying a large backpack in the village. Lynne just could not believe what I told her and seemed to be in a state of disbelief! I eventually managed to escape from the clutches of inquisitive people I knew, and carried on down Harbour Road on the genuine final, final leg of my journey. I strode past the ice-house and the early 19th Century harbour itself, without noticing any aches or pains, as I was on cloud nine at nearing completion.

I walked to the end of the River Brora and took my final photo of its outflow into the Moray Firth and the North Sea beyond. It was 6.00 and I had finally completed my journey. I then sauntered across to the car park to the waiting throngs of Jacqui and my Mum, and Jacquie's Mum and Dad. I posed for a photo, for the record, of me at the end of my expedition (Plate 24) and, in a way, could hardly believe it was all over. It was a curiously strange finalé to the trip. I wanted to celebrate with a beer, but I had got quite chilled stopping a few times over the last half mile and the wind at the exposed coastal edge was bitingly cold. So, after a brief welcome, I took off my rucksack, loaded it into the car and I sat down on a seat for the first time in a week!

I'd been thinking for a few days about what I would like to eat on completion of my expedition. I'd decided that fish and chips would just fit the bill completely! As we drove to the chip shop in neighbouring Golspie, I found it quite difficult to relate to Jacquie and my Mum, there and then, my experiences of the past week, as they were all so inter-twined in my mind. Sure, I could tell of individual, isolated happenings and sightings, such as the otter, or the white lousewort, or the views from the top of this hill or that, but because it was really a narrative, a continually unravelling adventure, there was little I felt I could say in a casual conversational way. I suppose it was a bit of an anti-climax, as the end of anything significant always seems to be, and this is the real reason that this narrative has been put down on paper; it just seemed to be the best way to tell the whole story – for family, friends or anyone else who happens to read this far!

During those seven magnificent days, I experienced many highs, very few lows and a whole series of joined-up, above average times, which all combined to give me the best 'Boy's Own' adventure I could have possibly wished for, in what was really my own back yard. I saw some sights which I may *never* see again. The whole experience cost me only the price of the petrol to Durness and a few packets of food – around £20!!!

Sutherland truly is the most magnificent part of the country; a place where I have been so very fortunate enough to make my home. I *never* feel the need for a 'proper' holiday, as I feel that just being here *is* my holiday, especially when I can have an adventure like this on my doorstep. Before I came to Sutherland, driving home south, after spending many times in the Highlands, was pretty depressing, but now, actually living here, absorbing the culture and the natural beauty of the land, being part of the community, I feel as though I am on holiday – permanently!

GLOSSARY

Allt	River
Bealach	Low point on a ridge, acting as a pass between valleys
Ben/Beinn	Mountain
Burn	Stream
Cnoc	Hill
Coire	Large glacially-shaped bowl, often containing a lochan
Corn-drying kiln	Kiln used for drying grain, associated with farmstead or township
Croft	Small tenanted lot of agricultural ground
Loch	Lake
Lochan	Small lake
Longhouse	Standard house dwelling in township, up to 45m long, but only up to 5m wide
Munro	One of 283 Scottish mountains over 3000' (914.4m), first tabled by Rev Hugh Munro in 1891
Outshot	Small jut out from main building line on township house, usually longhouse

Peat hag	Area of erosion in peat, often like a small ravine
Shieling	Very small, basic dwelling remote from the parent township, inhabited by women and children where they tended livestock on higher grazing during the summer months
Strath/Srath	Valley
Township	Small settlement
Uisge Beatha	Gaelic for whisky, literally 'water of life'
Whin	Gorse